Carol,
Remember, God
always keeps ♡
promises.
          Love,
      Ben + Shelly
        Christmas
          1999

His
Lady

Berkley Books by Bishop T. D. Jakes

The Lady, Her Lover, and Her Lord

His Lady

His Lady

Sacred Promises
for God's Woman

T. D. Jakes

BERKLEY BOOKS, NEW YORK

This book is an original publication of The Berkley Publishing Group.

HIS LADY

A Berkley Book
Published by The Berkley Publishing Group, a division of Penguin
Putnam Inc., 375 Hudson Street, New York, New York 10014.

First edition: September 1999

The Penguin Putnam Inc. World Wide Web site address is
http://www.penguinputnam.com

ISBN: 0-425-17287-2

BERKLEY®
Berkley Books are published by The Berkley Publishing Group,
a division of Penguin Putnam Inc.,
375 Hudson Street, New York, New York 10014.
BERKLEY and the "B" design are trademarks
belonging to Penguin Putnam Inc.

PRINTED IN THE UNITED STATES OF AMERICA
10 9 8 7 6 5 4 3 2 1

Contents

I WANT TO DEDICATE this book to all the women who have seen God's hand through prayer. I would like to dedicate this book to all the relentless women who have prayed up strength, prayed into blessings and prayed out of trouble. These women have nourished their children, nurtured their families and nestled us all in the strong warmth of their undying faith. May this book be a constant source that women go back to in order to remind themselves of the many tragedies, triumphs and trophies that accompany being His lady.

But most of all, this book is dedicated to my mother, Mrs. Odith P. Jakes, whose bright strength and strong will has weakened the grip of her affliction while it strengthened my faith in our Lord. In the presence of great peril, He has always proven that she was, in fact, His lady.

In that same tenacious spirit, may this book be the fuel that women like her need to face the many challenges that go along with being alive. Always remember, my sisters, you are the apple of His eye, the embodiment of His expectations, and the recipient of His awesome and powerful love.

Introduction

*L*IFE IS A BEAUTIFUL ROSE—lovely to behold and rich with a heady fragrance that delights and intoxicates. But all roses have thorns that can scratch us and cut us and make us bleed. Thorns are part of the rose, just as difficulties are part of life. We cry, we mourn, we suffer the unavoidable hardships that inevitably befall us.

As a woman of God, when you are stuck by the thorns of life, you should turn to our Lord. He will walk with you through troubles and tragedies, hassles and hardships. He will be there through the tears and the challenges, holding your hand and holding you up. He is constant and enduring in His love. He will help you in your time of need.

Perhaps you are thinking that you are undeserving of God's merciful kindness. Maybe you've sinned and feel ashamed and unworthy. My sisters, now more than ever I urge you to look to the Lord. You are His treasure, more precious than diamonds or emeralds, more valuable than all the riches in the world. And no matter how far you've fallen, He will pick you up and restore you to purity. He knows the pain and guilt you are feeling. He knows the sins that sully your heart. But He sent you His Son, Jesus Christ, who made the way for you to be clean again. He took your sins and indiscretions and crucified them on the Cross. He forgives you, and wants you to forgive yourself. He loves you—You are His lady.

God made a promise to you. Read the Bible and know that He will always be with you. No matter what you're experiencing now, He will see you through. No matter how much you have sinned, He will redeem you. For whatever ails you, God has the cure. Look through the following pages for the vows the Lord has made to you. Seek comfort in His words. He is your refuge in the storm you are walking through.

The Power of Prayer

Have faith in the promises God made you, and in your times of need appeal to Him in prayer. Jesus said, "Whatever things you ask when you pray, believe that you receive them and you will have them" (Mark 11:24). Open your heart and passionately pray for God's assistance. Ask and you shall receive. Lift up your voice and cry out so that you may be heard.

The Lord says, "And send for skillful wailing women, that they may come" (Jeremiah 9:17). Wailing Women means praying women—women who pray openly and unashamedly. Strip away your self-consciousness and bare your soul to the Lord. Walk the streets, scream from the rooftops, proudly and unabashedly call on Jesus and He will come.

Humble yourself. Cry out and have no concern for what others think. It doesn't matter. It's none of their business. This is a one-on-one with your Father. Show God you are passionate in your prayers. Shout out and refuse to be silenced. Shout out and *never* shut up!

Answer the Lord's call—become a Wailing Woman! Throw yourself on the altar and ask that Jesus Christ come into your life and into your heart to see you through the dark times. Cry through the night, and remember, "Weeping may endure for a night, but joy comes in the morning" (Psalm 30:5). Wail for Him and daylight will surely come.

Wailing Women and the Wailing Wall

Recently, I had the wonderful opportunity to visit the Wailing Wall in Jerusalem. I have to tell you, I wasn't prepared for the movement of God that stormed my soul. I wept like a child at the Wailing Wall. I can't explain it. There were Orthodox Jews standing beside Muslims who were standing next to Christians. And they were all praying. It was the most awesome presence of God.

The stones of the wall date back to the ancient temples of the scriptures, where once the presence of God was manifest in a cloud of glory. This wall has withstood wars and conflicts, adversity and attacks. It is symbolic of the great strength of prayer, which is even more resilient than the wall itself.

With the same urgency that Jeremiah called for the women of mourning, I call you to form a praying wall of defense against the conflicts of life. Use prayer power to shield yourself from the troubles that can overwhelm you. Be strong in your prayers and protect yourself from the adversity that threatens to take you farther from God.

THE TROUBLES AND TROPHIES OF WAILING WOMEN

Another thing I noticed at the Wailing Wall is that Israelites write their prayers on tiny pieces of paper, roll them up and slip them into the crevices of the wall. They do this because they believe that the prayers then go straight to God.

Likewise, you should write down your prayers. When you write your prayers, you release them to God—you let them go so that He can do something with them. In the back of this book, you will find pages on which you can write your petitions. Pour out your heart. Pick up your pen and put down the words that express exactly what you need.

You will also find Trophy Pages. It is here that you should record prayers that have been answered. Consider answered prayers the trophies God bestows upon you for persevering in your faith and keeping strong in times of trouble. Give thanks to the Lord and acknowledge His gift to you. Let these pages serve as a reminder that God always keeps his promises to His lady.

God's Gift

When someone gives you a gift, you are naturally very grateful. You say thank you and perhaps write a thank-you note. When a gift is something so special, so amazing, your thankfulness might be so great that you also keep a special place for the giver in your heart.

God's unconditional love is such a gift. You should show your thanks through both words and deeds. Commit yourself to the Lord. Promise Him that you will keep Him in your heart, so that all you say and all you do reflects His goodness and His glory.

Throughout this little book, you will find vows you can make to the Lord. Close your eyes and lift your face to your Savior, speaking these words and making these promises. These vows may seem insignificant when compared to the generous gift of God's love, but prayer, praise and positive action are the only ways we can give thanks.

God promises you so much. Don't you think you should make promises to Him in return? Exchange vows with the Lord. Let God be your Spiritual Husband. He will be by your side, in good times and in bad, in sickness and in health, for richer or for poorer.

He will be your Lord, and you will forever be His lady.

His
Lady

Abandonment

Where can I go from Your Spirit?
Or where can I flee from Your presence?
If I ascend into heaven. You are there;
If I make my bed in hell, behold, You are
    there.
If I take the wings of the morning,
And dwell in the uttermost parts of the
    sea,
Even there Your hand shall lead me,
And Your right hand shall hold me.

(PSALM 139:7–10)

"Never will I leave you;
never will I forsake you."

(HEBREWS 13:5*)

Praise be to God,
   who has not rejected my
      prayer
   or withheld his love from
      me!

(PSALM 66:20*)

Fathers are all too often absent. Mothers leave their babies to be cared for by others. Husbands go out and never return. Everyday someone leaves and another is left languishing in their absence—alone, frightened, feeling abandoned.

But remember, God will never leave you. In good times and in bad, He is by your side. He is the Father who will always care for His children, the spiritual Husband who knows how to treat a woman. The Lord is with you always. You are never alone. God made His promise to you. He will always be there: in sickness and in health, through good times and in bad, for richer or for poor. And in death you will not part, but will be together forever in His holy embrace.

YOUR VOW TO GOD . . .

In my darkest hour, when everyone has left me and I feel utterly alone, I will remember that You are with me. I am Your daughter. I am Your lady. I am secure in the knowledge that You will always be by my side.

"Bring my soul out of prison,
That I may praise Your name;
The righteous shall sourround me,
For You shall deal bountifully with me."

(PSALM 142:7)

And pray that we may be delivered from wicked and evil men,
for not everyone has faith. But the Lord is faithful and he will
strengthen and protect you from the evil one.

(2 THESSALONIANS 3:2–3*)

You are my hiding place;
    you will protect me from
        trouble
    and surround me with
        songs of deliverance.

(PSALM 32:7*)

Sometimes those you love hurt you. Whether intentional or not, their sharp words, or sharp blows, pierce your heart and shatter your spirit. You feel damaged by their abuse. You feel helpless against their attack.

But the truth is there is something more powerful than their curses and their fists. Our Lord has promised to stand against your enemies and protect you. He has the power to restore you. What others break, Jesus can mend and make pure. He will never leave you.

Your vow to God . . .

Although others hurt me, all I have to do is turn to You and I will be comforted. You heal me and make me whole. I open my heart to You so You can protect it.

ddiction

It seems to be a fact of life that when I want to do what is right, I inevitably do what is wrong. I love God's law with all my heart. But there is another law at work within me that is at war with my mind. This law wins the fight and makes me a slave to the sin that is still within me. Oh, what a miserable peron I am! Who will free me from this life that is dominated by sin? Thank God! The answer is in Jesus Christ our Lord.

(ROMANS 7:21–25⁺)

Though we are slaves, our God has not deserted us in our bondage. He has shown us kindness in the sight of the kings of Persia: He has granted us new life to rebuild the house of our God and repair its ruins, and he has given us a wall of protection in Judah and Jerusalem.

(EZRA 9:9*)

> You have made known to
>   me the path of life;
> You will fill me with joy in
>   your presence,
> with eternal pleasures at
>   your right hand.

(PSALM 16:11*)

You have given yourself over to your addiction and it now controls you. You feel helpless, hopeless and held hostage by self-defeating behaviors. You want to be free, but you are held prisoner by what you believe you cannot overcome.

The good news is that if you turn your addiction over to Jesus Christ, He will lead you to freedom. He will tear down the walls of your prison and loosen the chains that bind you. He will free you, forgive you, heal you and restore you. Let Christ live in you, and He will give you new life. His love is stronger than your addiction.

YOUR VOW TO GOD . . .

I want You to take hold of my life, Jesus. I now let You free me from everything that imprisons me. I trust You, and let Your love guide me.

nger

When God saw that they had put a stop to their evil ways, he had mercy on them and didn't carry out the destruction he had threatened.

(JONAH 3:10+)

But now is the time to get rid of anger, rage, malicious behavior, slander, and dirty language.

(COLOSSIANS 3:8+)

For God decided to save us through our Lord Jesus Christ, not to pour out his anger on us.

(1 THESSALONIANS 5:9+)

Someone has done you wrong, and your first reaction is one of rage. The blood begins to pound in your head as the anger rises within you. You want to lash out and inflict the same kind of pain that has been inflicted upon you.

Wait! What are you doing? Do you really want to be like the person who hurt you? What would Jesus do? You know He would turn the other cheek. "But it's not fair!" you scream. "What about justice?" What about it? It's not for you to judge. There is only one judge, and you must trust in Him. Ask God to help you release your anger so that you may be like His Son. Turn the other cheek and forgive the one who has done you wrong.

YOUR VOW TO GOD . . .

Oh God, I am angry, but help me let it go. I will choose to be merciful and forgive the one who angered me. Thank You for giving me the strength to forgive and to follow in the steps of Jesus.

Anxiety

The righteous cry out, and
    the Lord hears them;
    he delivers them from all
    their troubles.

(PSALM 34:17*)

Have no fear of sudden
    disaster
    or of the ruin that
    overtakes the wicked,
for the Lord will be your
    confidence
    and will keep your foot
    from being snared.

(PROVERBS 3:25–26*)

Do not be anxious about anything, but in everything, by prayer and petition, with thanksgiving, present your requests to God. And the peace of God, which transcends all under-standing, will guard your hearts and your minds in Jesus Christ.

(PHILIPPIANS 4:6–7*)

Anxiety is fear that washes over you and stops you in your tracks. It paralyzes you and takes away everything good in your life. You let it take control until you can do nothing, say nothing and feel like you are nothing.

But you are something in the eyes of the Lord. He loves you and He cherishes you. What are you afraid of? Don't you know your Father is with you? With every step you take, you are accompanied by the Lord. If you should stumble, He will catch you. If you should fall, He will lift you up. And if you walk with Him, you will never lose your way. You are given the gift of God's grace, and that should give you the security to move ahead fearlessly.

When my mind is troubled and I feel like giving up, I turn to You and Your promises sing in me. I let You calm my spirit, and bring me peace. I hold on to You.

pathy

And let us consider how we may spur one another on toward love and good deeds. Let us not give up meeting together, as some are in the habit of doing, but let us encourage one another—and all the more as you see the Day approaching.

(HEBREWS 10:24–25*)

Do not merely listen to the word, and so deceive yourselves. Do what it says.

(JAMES 1:22*)

I pray that you may be active in sharing your faith, so that you will have a full understanding of every good thing we have in Christ.

(PHILEMON 1:6*)

Sometimes you stumble, sometimes you fall. Sometimes you don't move at all. You are lifeless, listless and lacking feelings of any kind. It is at those times that you feel like you will never feel God's power in your life again.

Don't give up! Don't let apathy turn you away from the life that the Lord wants you to have. He wants you to be a woman of action. He wants you to be a woman of passion. He wants you to want Him so badly that you'll climb the tallest mountain or cross the widest sea to be with Him. I know right now you don't think you have the energy, but look to God. Take steps—small steps leading to large steps—every day toward God, and He will take ten steps toward you for every one of yours.

YOUR VOW TO GOD . . .

Whenever I feel uninspired, whenever I don't feel anything at all, I just need to remember that if I only look toward You, You will fill me with Your passion and compassion. I am alive in Your love!

Betrayal

"Be strong and courageous. Do not be afraid or terrified because of them, for the Lord your God goes with you; he will never leave you nor forsake you."

(DEUTERONOMY 31:6*)

> Teach me your way,
>   O Lord;
>   lead me in a straight path
>   because of my oppressors.
> Do not turn me over to the
>   desire of my foes,
>   for false witnessses rise up
>   against me,
>   breathing out violence.
> I am still confident of this:
>   I will see the goodness of
>   the Lord
>   in the land of the living.

(PSALM 27:11–13*)

So we say with confidence,

> "The Lord is my helper; I
>   will not be afraid.
>   What can man do to me?"

(HEBREWS 13:6*)

When the trust you have placed in the hands of others is betrayed, you feel angry, hurt and disillusioned. You want to hurt them back, you want to cry out against their injustice.

But cry out, instead, to the Lord your God. Ask Him to help you forgive those who have turned on you. It's when you think you can never trust again that you must place your faith in God and let Him bring you restoration. He is faithful, He is good, He will never betray you.

YOUR VOW TO GOD . . .

I am hurt, but I will not let this destroy my faith in You. I know that You are faithful. I need to forgive those who have betrayed me, and I will do so in Your name. I will trust You always.

Bitterness

Make every effort to live in peace with all men and to be holy; without holiness no one will see the Lord. See to it that no one misses the grace of God and that no bitter root grows up to cause trouble and defile many.

(HEBREWS 12:14–15*)

Therefore, as God's chosen people, holy and dearly loved, clothe yourselves with compassion, kindness, humility, gentleness and patience. Bear with each other and forgive whatever grievances you may have against one another. Forgive as the Lord forgave you. And over all these virtues put on love, which binds them all together in perfect unity.

(COLOSSIANS 3:12–14*)

Get rid of all bitterness, rage, anger, harsh words, and slander, as well as all types of malicious behavior. Instead, be kind to each other, tenderhearted, forgiving one another, just as God through Christ has forgiven you.

(EPHESIANS 4:31–32+)

The bitter tree bears no fruit. It withers and dies because there is nothing to nourish it. Similarly, when you plant the seed of bitterness in your heart, no love can grow there, only thorns. The bitter heart is weak, it makes life unbearable.

The love of Christ is so sweet. It can bring life back to your barren existence, and before you know it, the fruit of His love will abound in your life. Sow the seeds of His love, and you will never be hungry again.

YOUR VOW TO GOD . . .

I release all the bitter roots that have taken hold in my life. I give them to You, knowing that You will replace them with the living seeds of Your love. I gratefully eat generously of Your fruit.

We hear that some among you are idle. They are not busy; they are busybodies. Such people we command and urge in the Lord Jesus Christ to settle down and earn the bread they eat. And as for you, brothers, never tire of doing what is right.

(2 THESSALONIANS 3:11–13*)

His divine power has given us everything we need for life and godliness through our knowledge of him who called us for his own glory and goodness. Through these he has given us his very great and precious promises, so that through them you may participate in the divine nature and escape the corruption in the world caused by evil desires.

(2 PETER 1:3–4*)

You will show me the path of life;
In Your presence *is* fullness of joy;
At Your right hand *are* pleasures
forevermore.

(PSALM 16:11)

Boredom is like being asleep. It's like being in a deep slumber and numb to all the beauty and joy of life. You are dozing when you should be doing.

Wake up! God is calling you for His purpose. He has a divine plan for you, and you must open your eyes and shake off that drowsiness. You must fully participate in the life God has given you. See His glory in everything in your life and get excited. Celebrate the gifts! Get on your feet! Praise Him! Be alive!

YOUR VOW TO GOD . . .

I will hear Your call, and wake up. I will feel Your life course through my body and my spirit, and I will become fully alive in Your love.

Conflict

Anyone who claims to be in the light but hates his brother is still in darkness. Whoever loves his brother lives in the light, and there is nothing in him to make him stumble. But whoever hates his brother is in the darkness and walks around in the darkness; he does not know where he is going, because the darkness has blinded him.

(1 JOHN 2:9–11*)

What is causing the quarrels and fights among you? Isn't it the whole army of evil desires at war within you? You want what you don't have, so you scheme and kill to get it. You are jealous for what others have, and you can't possess it, so you fight and quarrel to take it away from them. And yet the reason you don't have what you want is that you don't ask God for it.

(JAMES 4:1–2+)

> Whoever of you loves life
> and desires to see many
> good days,
> keep our tongue from evil
> and your lips from
> speaking lies.
> Turn from evil and do
> good;
> seek peace and pursue it.
>
> (PSALM 34:12–14*)

Conflict can feel like a war in your life. You're in battle with others—or maybe yourself—but the harder you fight, the more you lose. Arguments drain you of your valuable energy. Disagreements bring hurt and resentment. You struggle with who's wrong and who's right, and you spend so much time trying to out-do, out-shout and out-maneuver that you're about to go out of your mind.

End the war! Surrender! Surrender yourself to God and let Him lead you to peace. Let the love of Jesus fill you up so much that it overflows onto others. Let His mercy and His kindness course through you so that you too can be merciful and kind. He will bring tranquility to your life. Let Him guide you.

YOUR VOW TO GOD . . .

I put down my sword and allow You, the God of peace, to rule in my life. Only the serenity of the Lord will bring clarity out of this chaos. I trust You to guide me to Your purpose.

Confusion

We know also that the Son of God has come and has given us understanding, so that we may know him who is true. And we are in him who is true—even in his Son Jesus Christ. He is the true God and eternal life.

(1 JOHN 5:20*)

But it is the spirit in a man,
    the breath of the Almighty,
    that gives him
        understanding.

(JOB 32:8*)

Therefore, prepare your minds for action; be self-controlled; set your hope fully on the grace to be given you when Jesus Christ is revealed.

(1 PETER 1:13*)

The storm of chaos swirls around you. Darkness surrounds you and you reach out blindly, grasping at air, feeling lost. You are overwhelmed and under pressure. You don't know which way to turn, so you walk aimlessly in circles. You just want to sit down, put your head in your hands and cry.

Yet the clouds will part and God will shine His heavenly light to lead you. Bask in the warmth of His love and know that clarity comes to you if you just reach out your hand to Him. He will give you understanding. He will speak to your heart. He will guide you out of the darkness.

YOUR VOW TO GOD . . .

When I am lost and wandering, unsure of what I should do, I only have to lift up my face toward You, my Lord, and You will gently lead me. You are the light. You are my beacon. I will stay focused on You.

Covetousness

"You shall not covet your
  neighbor's house;
  you shall not covet your neighbor's
  wife, nor his male servant,
  nor his
  female servant, nor
  his ox, nor his
  donkey, nor
  anything that *is* your neighbor's."
(EXODUS 20:17)

You want something but you don't get it. You kill and covet,
but you cannot have what you want. You quarrel and fight.
You do not have because you do not ask God.
(JAMES 4:2*)

His divine power has given us everything we need for life and
godliness through our knowledge of him who called us by his
own glory and goodness. Through these he has given us his
very great and precious promises, so that through them you
may participate in the divine nature and escape the corruption
in the world caused by evil desires.
(2 PETER 1:3–4*)

God has told us that desiring what others have is a sin. It leads to an empty life because you don't appreciate what you already have. God has already blessed you, but when you covet, you are being disrespectful of the gifts He has given you.

Begin to count the many blessing in your life. See the bountiful table set before you. Look all around you and recognize the gifts that have been placed in your hands. Instead of wanting what others have, show appreciation for what *you* have. Give your thanks to our generous God. Praise Him and let Him lead you from a place of desperation and despair to a life full of joy and abundance.

Your vow to God . . .

My life is full of blessings from You. I shall not want anything other than what You want for me. I am totally satisfied.

Cynicism

Many are asking, "Who can
   show us any good?"
Let the light of your face
   shine upon us, O Lord.
You have filled my heart
   with greater joy
than when their grain and
   new wine abound.
I will lie down and sleep in
   peace,
      for you alone, O Lord,
      make me dwell in safety.

(PSALM 4:6–8*)

He who seeks good finds good will,
   but evil comes to him who
      searches for it.

(PROVERBS 11:27*)

David said about him:
   "I saw the Lord always
      before me.
   Because he is at my right
      hand,
   I will not be shaken.
   Therefore my heart is glad
      and my tongue rejoices;
   my body also will live in
      hope."

(ACTS 2:25–26*)

A black cloud envelops you. Everything looks hopeless and dreary. There is no bright side; your dismal outlook colors everything in shades of gray. You're cynical about everything and everybody, always thinking the worst and expecting the least. Cynicism is the belief that God will forsake you. You fear that His promises aren't real, so you guard your heart with sharp words and negative thoughts.

But in the beginning *was* the Word, and God keeps His word. You can rely totally on Him because He made you from the first and will be there with you to the last. Let Him bring light in to your day so you can see the world in all its brilliance. Trust that He is always with you and the sunshine of His love will shine brightly on you.

YOUR VOW TO GOD . . .

I totally and completely loose the shackles of fear, distrust, and negativity that bind my heart. You have set me free. I believe Your promises. I am Your lady.

Death

Don't be afraid! I am the First and the Last. I am the living one who died. Look, I am forever and ever! And I hold the keys of death and the grave.

(REVELATION 1:17B–18⁺)

For none of us lives to himself alone and none of us dies to himself alone. If we live, we live to the Lord; and if we die, we die to the Lord. So, whether we live or die, we belong to the Lord.

For this very reason, Christ died and returned to life so that he might be the Lord of both the dead and the living.

(ROMANS 14:7–9*)

> I know that my Redeemer
>   lives,
>   and that in the end he will
>   stand upon the earth.
> And after my skin has been
>   destroyed,
>   yet in my flesh I will see
>   God;

(JOB 19:25–26*)

I know you're hurting right now. You've lost someone you love and the grief cuts through you. You're not mourning your loved one's passing; you know that child of God is back with the Heavenly Father. No, you don't cry for the person you buried today. You cry for yourself, for your loss.

Now is the time that you need your Lord the most. Let Him comfort you and release the pain that pierces your heart. Let Him hold you in His arms and rock you as you shed your tears. It's okay to cry—you are hurting. But know that God will bring light to your darkness. Know that "Weeping may endure for a night, but joy *comes* in the morning" (Psalm 30:5). Have courage. It will soon be morning.

YOUR VOW TO GOD . . .

My Lord, I have lost someone I love and the pain is bitter and sharp. But I know that my loved one is now with You and that You will be with me to shepherd me through this difficult time. I will turn to You for comfort and have peace in the knowledge that You will bring me through this.

Denial

If we claim to be without sin, we deceive ourselves and the truth is not in us.

(1 JOHN 1:8*)

"Why do you look at the speck of sawdust in your brother's eye and pay no attention to the plank in your own eye? How can you say to your brother, 'Brother, let me take the speck out of your eye,' when you yourself fail to see the plank in your own eye? You hypocrite, first take the plank out of your eye, and then you will see clearly to remove the speck from your brother's eye."

(LUKE 6:41–42*)

For with the heart one believes unto righteousness, and with the mouth confession is made unto salvation.

(ROMANS 10:10)

There is no sin as fatal as not acknowledging your sins. She who confesses will be forgiven, but pity the woman who refuses to take responsibility for her wrong-doings. The Lord promises that if we confess He will redeem us. You must come face-to-face with the truth before the truth can set you free. It is only when you deliver up your flaws to God that He can wash them clean.

God desires your perfection and your purity. He wants to restore you. He sent His Son to save you; your sins and imperfections were crucified on the Cross. Lay your sins at Jesus' feet and accept His grace. Have no fear, you will be forgiven.

Your vow to God . . .

There are things in my life I am not proud of, things I want to hide. But I cannot hide from You, my Lord. I know if I step into the light of truth and offer up my sins, You will shine Your light in me.

Depression

"Come to me, all you who are weary and burdened, and I will give you rest. Take my yoke upon you and learn from me, for I am gentle and humble in your heart, and you will find rest for your souls. For my yoke is easy and my burden is light."

(MATTHEW 11:28–30*)

If I say, "Surely the darkness
        will hide me
    and the light become night
        around me,"
even the darkness will not be
        dark to you;
    the night will shine like the day,
    for darkness is as light to
            you.

(PSALM 139:11–12*)

"Then maidens will dance
        and be glad,
    young men and old as well.
I will turn their mourning
        into gladness;
    I will give them comfort
        and joy instead of sorrow.
I will satisfy the priests with
        abundance,
    and my people will be
        filled with my bounty,"
            declares the Lord.

(JEREMIAH 31:13–14*)

It can feel like you are lost in the blistering wind of a chaotic storm in your life. You feel like you have drifted into some dark place where no one can locate you. It is as if you are laying in a pit of pain and indecision and feel like you could die.

But through the pain comes the hand of God, which saves you from your misery. Know that you can stand with God. He will hold you up in troubled times. Because of His loving touch, you can and will survive.

Your vow to God . . .

What a relief to know there is a light that can shine through my darkness. You are a loving God that can find me and save me even in the depths of depression. I hold on to Your love, and allow You to sustain me. You alone can save me.

Despair

"Do not let your hearts be troubled. Trust in God; trust also in me."

(JOHN 14:1*)

> "He will call upon me, and I
>   will answer him;
> I will be with him in
>   trouble,
> I will deliver him and
>   honor him."

(PSALM 91:15*)

The Lord appeared to us in
the past, saying:

> "I have loved you with an
>   everlasting love;
> I have drawn you with
>   loving-kindness.
> I will build you up again
>   and you will be rebuilt,
>   O Virgin Israel.
> Again you will take up your
>   tambourines
>   and go out to dance with
>   the joyful."

(JEREMIAH 31:3–4*)

Sometimes you feel like there is no one to help you through your darkest nights. You cry out but hear no answers. You ache and feel no relief. You think that you are all alone, that no one can even understand how you feel.

God does. He knows every corner and crevice in your heart. He will shine His all-powerful light into your darkest areas and replace your despair with hope. Just have faith in Him. He will show you His mercy and His steadfast glory.

YOUR VOW TO GOD . . .

No longer will I believe I am alone. You are here with me now. You are my Savior. You love me. You help me. You fill me with hope. I am flooded with Your glory.

Desperation

The Spirit of the Sovereign Lord is on me,
    because the Lord has anointed me
    to preach good news to the poor.
He has sent me to bind up the brokenhearted,
    to proclaim freedom for the captives
    and release for the prisoners,
to proclaim the year of the Lord's favor
    and the day of vengeance of our God,
to comfort all who mourn.

(ISAIAH 61:1–2*)

I cry to you, O Lord;
    I say, "You are my refuge,
    my portion in the land of the living."
Listen to my cry,
    for I am in desperate need;
rescue me from those who pursue me,
    for they are too strong for me.

(PSALM 142:5–6 *)

On my bed I remember you;
    I think of you through the
        watches of the night.
Because you are my help,
    I sing in the shadow of
        your wings.
I stay close to you;
    your right hand upholds
        me.

(PSALM 63:6–8*)

Turbulent waters are washing over you, pushing you under, waves crashing in your face. You're thrashing your arms and kicking your legs, but the harder you fight the farther down the water pulls you. You're gasping for air and grasping for life, but it seems all your efforts are in vain.

Stop and trust in the Lord. Be secure in the knowledge that He will never let you drown. He is your life raft even in the stormiest sea. Surrender yourself to His mercy and let His arms bring you to safety.

YOUR VOW TO GOD . . .

In my darkest times, when I think I can't take anymore, I will instead give: I will give myself over to You, my Heavenly Father. And I will give thanks to You because You saved me.

Disappointment

Therefore we do not lose heart. Though outwardly we are wasting away, yet inwardly we are being renewed day by day. For our light and momentary troubles are achieving for us an eternal glory that far outweighs them all. So we fix our eyes not on what is seen, but on what is unseen. For what is seen is temporary, but what is unseen is eternal.

(2 Corinthians 4:16–17*)

And hope does not disappoint us, because God has poured out his love into our hearts by the Holy Spirit, whom he has given us.

(Romans 5:5*)

They cried to you and were
    saved;
  in you they trusted and
    were not disappointed.

(Psalm 22:5*)

You feel disappointed by someone or something, and it hurts deep and hard. You keep thinking of how it could have been or how that person let you down. It's as if you've forgotten that God is in control. Disappointment can make you hard, turn you to stone.

The cure for disappointment is knowing that God knows you and has prepared for you a majestic life filled with the riches of His love and the pearls of His peace. He is the Master Giver. Once you know Him you can never truly want for anything again.

YOUR VOW TO GOD . . .

I give my disappointment to You, my Lord, knowing that You will remind me of Your holy vows to me. I love You and let You adorn me with the jewels of Your love.

Disbelief

Jesus said to her, "Did I not say to you that if you would believe you would see the glory of God?"

(JOHN 11:40)

He then brought them out and asked, "Sirs, what must I do to be saved?"

They replied, "Believe in the Lord Jesus, and you will be saved—you and your household."

(ACTS 16:30–31*)

And when He had come into the house, the blind men came to Him. And Jesus said to them, "Do you believe that I am able to do this?" They said to Him, "Yes, Lord."

Then He touched their eyes saying, "According to your faith let it be to you."

And their eyes were opened.

(MATTHEW 9:28–30A)

What causes you to question God's glory? What trouble makes you doubt His grace? Oh, I know it must have been something horrible, something so terrible you couldn't bear it. So you closed your eyes. But now you're blind, fumbling in the darkness, feeling lost and alone.

I know you want to regain your sight. All you need to do is believe and just as when Jesus laid His hands on the blind man's eyes, your vision will be restored. Believe, and even in your despair you will see God's glorious light and will find meaning in what seems meaningless. You will find comfort in His holy embrace.

YOUR VOW TO GOD . . .

My Lord, my Savior, I trust in Your divine plan and know You are here for me. I place my unwavering belief in You and bask in Your glory.

Dishonesty

The man of integrity walks
    securely,
  but he who takes crooked
    paths will be found out.
(PROVERBS 10:9*)

"These are the things you are to do: Speak the truth to each other, and render true and sound judgment in your courts; do not plot evil against your neighbor, and do not love to swear falsely. I hate all this," declares the Lord.
(ZECHARIAH 8:16–17*)

Therefore each of you must put off falsehood and speak truthfully to his neighbor, for we are all members of one body.
(EPHESIANS 4:25*)

When you've been dishonest, the guilt can make you feel like you are forever unworthy of God's love and trust again. You may feel like you've betrayed Him with your lies, and that you've used up your last chance.

Start telling the truth now! You can undo crimes of the past by laying the foundation of the future with today's honesty. God is our only chance. Our Lord set us free with His truth. He came to set the record straight and you must trust Him above all else. He is the revealer of lies and the restorer of life.

YOUR VOW TO GOD . . .

I promise to live with truth, the whole truth, and nothing but His truth. I pledge to be honest to Him . . . and to myself.

Distraction

Let your eyes look straight
    ahead,
     fix your gaze directly
     before you.
Make level paths for your
    feet
     and take only the ways that are
     firm.
Do not swerve to the right
    or the left;
     keep your foot from evil.

(PROVERBS 4:25–27*)

Dear children, do not let anyone lead you astray. He who does what is right is righteous.

(1 JOHN 3:7*)

Therefore, since we are surrounded by such a great cloud of witnesses, let us throw off everything that hinders and the sin that so easily entangles, and let us run with perseverance the race marked out for us. Let us fix our eyes on Jesus, the author and perfecter of our faith, who for the joy set before him endured the cross, scorning its shame, and sat down at the right hand of the throne of God.

(HEBREWS 12:1–2*)

Have you ever driven a car down a busy road and been distracted by something—perhaps a billboard or a conversation with a friend? Suddenly you see that you are about to hit the car in front of you, so you slam on the brakes and swerve to safety.to avoid a car wreck.

Are you distracted by situations and people in your life? "Life wrecks" can happen if you take your focus off God's will for you. He has designed you to be a smart, vital, fulfilled woman. Come and bring your focus back onto Him and watch how He will change your life.

YOUR VOW TO GOD . . .

I will keep my eyes on Your road and pay attention to the signs You give me. You have promised to lead me, and I promise to go where You lead.

Doubt

If you make the Most High
  your dwelling—
 even the Lord, who is my
  refuge—
then no harm will befall you,
  no disaster will come near
  your tent.
For he will command his
  angels concerning you
 to guard you in all your
  ways;
  they will lift you up in their
  hands,
  so that you will not strike
  your foot against a stone.

(PSALM 91:9–12*)

"Have faith in God," Jesus answered. "I tell you the truth, if anyone says to this mountain, 'Go, throw yourself into the sea,' and does not doubt in his heart but believes that what he says will happen, it will be done for him. Therefore I tell you, whatever you ask for in prayer, believe that you have received it, and it will be yours."

(MARK 11:22–24*)

Know therefore that the Lord your God is God; he is the faithful God, keeping his covenant of love to a thousand generations of those who love him and keep his commands.

(DEUTERONOMY 7:9*)

Doubt is a cancer on the heart of His lady. It starts small, just a little dark dot that you hardly notice, but soon it grows into a full-blown disease. Then it takes control and dictates how you live your life—moving you from a woman of faith to a woman of fear. It diminishes you until you become a mere shell of who the Lord has called you to be.

What you need to know is that He doesn't doubt you. God believes in you as the woman He created, the woman He already knows you to be. Ask the Lord to bring you from doubt to trust, from fear to faith.

YOUR VOW TO GOD . . .

Doubt has been eating away at me for a long time. I believe in You, and I know that You believe in me. I turn my doubt in You into my duty for You.

Emptiness

May the God of hope fill you with all joy and peace as you trust in him, so that you may overflow with hope by the power of the Holy Spirit.

(ROMANS 15:13*)

If you extend your soul to the hungry
And satisfy the afflicted soul,
Then your light shall dawn in the darkness,
And your darkness shall *be* as the
    noonday.
The Lord will guide you continually,
And satisfy your soul in drought,
And strengthen your bones;
You shall be like a watered garden,
And like a spring of water, whose waters
    do not fall.

(ISAIAH 58:10–11)

Trust in the Lord and do
    good;
    dwell in the land and enjoy
    safe pasture.
Delight yourself in the
    Lord
    and he will give you the
    desires of your heart.

(PSALM 37:3–4*)

You ache. You want to reach out for someone—anyone—to help you, to bring you back from the empty pit that has become your prison. But you don't have the strength to lift up your hand. You feel like you're alone, afraid, parched and dying.

You've felt empty long enough. I ask you to call out to the Holy Spirit—whisper if that's all you can do. He'll hear you because He's already there, and He's cradling you right now. *Phew!* Doesn't it change everything to know that you are not alone? Life—God's life in you—is suddenly worth living again.

GOD'S VOW TO YOU . . .

God, You are here with me now and You are not silent. You speak to me and shatter the deafening emptiness to let me know that I am Your beloved. You will never forget or forsake me. My emptiness is filled with Your incredible love.

Envy

A heart at peace gives life to
  the body,
 but envy rots the bones.

(PROVERBS 14:30*)

But if you harbor bitter envy and selfish ambition in your hearts, do not boast about it or deny the truth. Such "wisdom" does not come down from heaven but is earthly, unspiritual, of the devil.

(JAMES 3:14–15*)

Therefore, rid yourselves of all malice and deceit, hypocrisy, envy, and slander of every kind. Like newborn babies, crave pure spiritual milk, so that by it you may grow up in your salvation.

(1 PETER 2:1–2*)

Few feelings are more destructive than envy—that constant comparing of yourself to that woman you work with or to that model on the magazine cover. Envy is a game, and once you play that game you can find something to envy everywhere you look. There will always be someone who is younger, thinner or richer.

God, however, does not compare you to anyone. He looks at you and truly sees *you*. He knows the desires of your heart and the thoughts of your mind. He doesn't want you to be better than (or worse than) anyone else, only the best you can be. Isn't that a relief? He made you totally unique—His lovely creation. God sees the real you, and He is pleased.

YOUR VOW TO GOD . . .

Lord, You created me to be Your unique lady. I don't have to compare myself to anyone else because I am so busy learning who You want me to be. I turn any old thoughts of envy into an opportunity to love others as they are, and to love myself as I am and as I am becoming.

Evil

The Lord loves the righteous.
The Lord watches over the strangers;
He relieves the fatherless and widow;
But the way of the wicked He turns upside
    down.

(PSALM 146:8B–9)

The fear of the Lord *leads* to life,
And *he who has it* will abide in
    satisfaction;
He will not be visited with evil.

(PROVERBS 19:23)

Do not say, "I will recompense evil";
Wait for the Lord, and He will save you.

(PROVERBS 20:22)

Evil. Just the word sounds nasty and mean. Evil people can do evil things and cause havoc, confusion, even danger. Sometimes the devil can even get us to do things we don't want to do through his sly ways. I sometimes picture myself holding up the shield of Jesus in front of me to hold back the evil that's coming toward me. It can almost feel like too much.

It's fascinating to notice, however, that the word "evil" spelled backward is "live." When we live in God's word and do what He desires us to do, we are promised by God to be protected. He guarantees it. There is no power greater than God's, and He protects us from all evil.

Your vow to God . . .

I cloak myself in Your words and Your promises. You deliver me from evil and free me from worry. I will not fear anyone or anything, for You are on my side.

Exhaustion

You will be secure, because
    there is hope;
  you will look about you
  and take your rest in
    safety.

(JOB 11:18*)

You, O Lord, keep my lamp
    burning;
  my God turns my darkness
    into light.
With your help I can
    advance against a troop;
  with my God I can scale a wall.

(PSALM 18:28–29*)

I have fought the good fight, I have finished the race, I have
kept the faith. Now there is in store for me the crown of righteousness, which the Lord, the righteous Judge, will award to
me on that day—and not only to me, but also to all who have
longed for his appearing.

(2 TIMOTHY 4:7–8*)

Living life can feel like running a long-distance marathon. You race from the kids to work to home, where you cook, clean, pay the bills and pray it all holds together. And those seem like the good days. No wonder you're exhausted. You're running as fast as you can, and yet you still feel like you're not doing enough.

I have a thought about you: Maybe you are too busy *not* to stop and give it all to Jesus. He made a promise to You that I think you'll want to know about. Jesus said that all who are weary should give their lives to Him and He'll make their burdens light. He won't give us more than we can do, and the best part is that we can rest in Him. He is the healing tonic that restores and renews your parched spirit. When you can't run anymore, He will carry you.

Your vow to God . . .

I'm tired of being tired. Jesus, help me to go from just running around to running toward something—You. I am Your lady, and I will not live my life in vain. I dedicate everything I do today and everyday to You and the healing love You have for me.

xploitation

And above all things have fervent love for one another, for *"love will cover a multitude of sins."*

Be hospitable to one another without grumbling.

As each one has received a gift, minister it to one another, as good stewards of the manifold grace of God.

(1 Peter 4:8–10)

God is not unjust; he will not forget your work and the love you have shown him as you have helped his people and continue to help them.

(Hebrews 6:10*)

Serve wholeheartedly, as if you were serving the Lord, not men, because you know that the Lord will reward everyone for whatever good he does, whether he is a slave or free.

(Ephesians 6:7–8*)

You're feeling used, abused and thrown away like yesterday's news. You thought they liked you—even loved you—but now you find they were just using you for their own advantage. That's what happens when you put your life in the hands of mere mortals. They are not creators; they can't make anything out of you. They can only use you.

Instead, put your life in the gentle and protective hands of God. He is the only Creator, and the only thing He wants to make out of you is you. He *is* using you for His own purpose, but that purpose is for you to be a woman of excellence. Let God use you . . . to be an instrument of His love.

YOUR VOW TO GOD . . .

Oh Lord, protect me from those who want to take advantage of me. I only want to be used by You. I offer myself to You. Please use me for Your good.

Failure

And the God of all grace, who called you to his eternal glory in Christ, after you have suffered a little while, will himself restore you and make you strong, firm and steadfast.

(1 PETER 5:10*)

Do not gloat over me, my enemy!
Though I have fallen, I
will rise.
Though I sit in darkness,
the Lord will be my
light.
Because I have sinned
against him,
I will bear the Lord's
wrath,
until he pleads my case
and establishes my right.
He will bring me out into
the light;
I will see his justice.

(MICAH 7:8–9*)

The Lord upholds all those
who fall
and lifts up all who are
bowed down.

(PSALM 145:14*)

Sometimes the road is bumpy. You stumble. You fall. You feel like a failure, and all you want to do is curl up in the corner and cry. It's like your heart is bruised and your soul is battered.

But dry your eyes, wipe away your tears. The Lord Jesus Christ will lift you up. Move toward Him—crawl if you have to—and ask Him to restore you. Reach out your hand and He will pull you to your feet. God doesn't want you to stay down. He doesn't think you are a failure. You are perfect in His eyes.

YOUR VOW TO GOD . . .

I will always try my best in whatever I do. But if I stumble, if I fall, I will trust that You, my Lord, will lift me up. I know You have a divine plan for me, and You want me to succeed. I am Your lady—I am always a winner in Your eyes.

Fear

There is no fear in love; but perfect love casts out fear, because fear involves torment. But he who fears has not been made perfect in love.

(1 JOHN 4:18)

But I will rescue you on that day, declares the Lord; you will not be handed over to those you fear.

(JEREMIAH 39:17*)

But now, thus says the Lord, who created
    you, O Jacob,
And He who formed you, O Israel:
"Fear not, for I have redeemed you;
I have called *you* by your name;
You *are* Mine.
When you pass through the waters, I *will*
    be with you;
And through the rivers, they shall not
    overflow you.
When you walk through the fire, you shall
    not be burned,
Nor shall the flame scorch you.

(ISAIAH 43:1–2)

You're frightened, like a child trembling in the dark, hiding under the covers, afraid of the monsters beneath her bed. If that little girl called to you in the night, scared and alone, you would comfort her. You'd tell her that there are no monsters and you are there for her, ready to protect her. You'd hold her in your arms and rock her to sleep, safe in your embrace.

Well, let me tell you, your Heavenly Father is here to calm your fears. Rest easy in the knowledge that He won't let anything hurt you. Take heart that even in your darkest moments, He will cradle you in His arms and sing softly to you. Sleep peacefully, little girl. God is always watching over you.

YOUR VOW TO YOURSELF . . .

Even when I am most afraid, I will remember that You are protecting me. You watch over me and let no harm come my way. I rest peacefully in Your arms. I am no longer afraid.

Financial Strain

"Give, and it will be given to you: good measure, pressed down, shaken together, and running over will be put into your bosom. For with the same measure that you use, it will be measured back to you."

(LUKE 6:38)

"Submit to God and be at
    peace with him;
  in this way prosperity will
    come to you.
Accept instruction from his
    mouth
  and lay up his words in
    your heart.
If you return to the
    Almighty, you will be
    restored:
  If you remove wickedness
    far from your tent
and assign your nuggets to
    the dust,
  your gold of Ophir to the
    rocks in the ravines,
then the Almighty will be
    your gold,
  the choicest silver for
    you."

(JOB 22:21–25*)

The rent is due, the bills are late and the tax collector is knocking at your door. You've been taught that the love of money is the root of all evil, but you're feeling that the lack of money is even worse. You're in debt and you just seem to fall farther behind every day.

Don't despair. God will take care of you. Trust that the difficulties of today are the down payment for a better tomorrow. God is preparing you for the glorious future He has in store for you. As His daughter, you will inherit His kingdom. Have patience. Wait upon the Lord. He will not forsake you.

YOUR VOW TO GOD . . .

Today I notice the riches in every area of my life. I see how generous You have been to me, and I trust You completely to bring forth even more abundance in my life.

Frustration

Brothers, as an example of patience in the face of suffering, take the prophets who spoke in the name of the Lord. As you know, we consider blessed above those who have persevered. You have heard of Job's perseverance and have seen what the Lord finally brought about. The Lord is full of compassion and mercy.

(JAMES 5:10–11*)

But these things I plan won't happen right away. Slowly, steadily, surely, the time approaches when the vision will be fulfilled. If it seems slow, wait patiently, for it will surely take place. It will not be delayed.

(HABAKKUK 2:3+)

You're frustrated. Things aren't working the way you want them to, and you're angry. It feels like no matter how hard you try, you're not getting what you want.

Doesn't that make you stop and think? Don't you ask yourself *why*? You know God wants the best for you, so maybe what you want isn't what you need. You're trying to direct the journey, but God has already set the path straight at your feet. Follow it. Trust Him and He will lead you. Stop trying to control things—stop struggling. Let go and let God take care of you.

YOUR VOW TO GOD . . .

I realize that what I want isn't necessarily what is best for me. Only You know what is best, and I trust You to deliver me to it. I will stop fighting right now and let You take me to my reward.

Futility

He replied, "Because you have so little faith. I tell you the truth, if you have faith as small as a mustard seed, you can say to this mountain, 'Move from here to there' and it will move. Nothing will be impossible for you."

(MATTHEW 17:20*)

Jesus replied, "What is impossible with men, is possible with God."

(LUKE 18:27*)

"For nothing is impossible with God."

(LUKE 1:37*)

In every gym, you're likely to find a treadmill. Step on, start running and . . . keep running. Funny thing is you can run for miles and not get anywhere; you're at the same physical spot where you started in the gym. But have you gotten anywhere? Chances are, if you run on that treadmill consistently, you will have a stronger heart, get fit and be healthier. You will see positive results.

Life is sometimes like a treadmill. You are doing so much, but you feel like it is all for naught. But know that your life is a vital piece of God's plan. Have faith that all you do serves His divine purpose. Your job is to follow the path God put you on. Do what is in front of you and God will do the rest. You *will* reap the rewards.

Your vow to God . . .

How can I think my life is useless when it is an instrument of Your will? I have purpose: I am here to do my Father's business.

Greed

Whoever loves money never
has money enough;
whoever loves wealth is
never satisfied with his
income.
This too is meaningless.

(ECCLESIASTES 5:10*)

But whoever has this world's goods, and sees his brother in need, and shuts up his heart from him, how does the love of God abide in him?

(1 JOHN 3:17)

Keep your lives free from the love of money and be content with what you have, because God has said,
"Never will I leave you;
never will I forsake you."

(HEBREWS 13:5*)

It's a fever that invades your mind. You want more and still more. When you let greed into your life, you are setting up an altar to false idols. For what is greed but the worship of material things and the love of money? You focus more on what you want than on what God has given you.

Put nothing before God, for He is the eternal treasure. What could be worth more than the glorious life that His love provides? When it comes to financial and material wealth: "Seek ye first the kingdom of God and everything else will be added unto you."

Your vow to God . . .

All the riches I want are already mine, for You are in my life. I now name You my financial planner. You will give me exactly what I need, when I need it.

Guilt

If we confess our sins, he is faithful and just and will forgive us our sins and purify us from all unrighteousness.

(1 JOHN 1:9*)

Then I acknowledged my sin
        to you
    and did not cover up my
        iniquity.
I said, "I will confess
    my transgressions to the
        Lord"—
and you forgave
    the guilt of my sin.

(PSALM 32:5*)

I have swept away your
        offenses like a cloud,
    your sins like the morning
        mist.
Return to me,
    for I have redeemed you."

(ISAIAH 44:22*)

You have sinned and you know it. You know you could have done better, but you didn't. And now the guilt infects you. It fills you with filth that rots you to the very core of your being.

Even though it may seem like it, all is not lost. Just confess your sins to the Almighty Lord and you will be forgiven. Invite Him in and He will wash away your guilt and return you to purity. He is good, He is faithful. He gives you the gift of forgiveness and now wants you to forgive yourself. Lay your sins at His feet. You are forgiven.

YOUR VOW TO GOD . . .

I have sinned, but You have promised that if I confess You will forgive me and make me new. I promise You in return to admit my wrongdoings and know that I will be restored.

Hardship

As you endure this divine discipline, remember that God is treating you as his own children. Whoever heard of a child who was never disciplined? . . . Since we respect our earthly fathers who disciplined us, should we not all the more cheerfully submit to the discipline of our heavenly Father and live forever?

For our earthly fathers disciplined us for a few years, doing the best they knew how. But God's discipline is always right and good for us because it means we will share in his holiness.

(HEBREWS 12:7, 9–10[+])

You have been a refuge for
            the poor,
        a refuge for the needy in
            his distress,
    a shelter from the storm
        and a shade from the heat.
For the breath of the
            ruthless
        is like a storm driving
            against a wall
        and like the heat of the
            desert.
You silence the uproar of
            foreigners;
        as heat is reduced by the
            shadow of a cloud,
        so the song of the ruthless
            is stilled.

(ISAIAH 25:4–5[*])

Hardship is an unwanted guest, but invite it into your home. Yes, you heard me right. When misfortune comes knocking at your door, bow your head and endure the visit with dignity. For although unpleasant, you are being sent a teacher. God would not let you suffer in vain—He is sending you a gift. Be ready to receive it.

You will endure this hardship. Jesus Christ is with you, and He is bringing a lesson. He is teaching you the way to holiness. He will see you through this difficulty and reward you with eternal life.

YOUR VOW TO GOD . . .

In these difficult times, instead of crying I will rejoice, for now I know I am one of Your children. You are preparing me for glorious things and I eagerly accept Your gift. I know You would not burden me with more than I can bear. I will survive this crisis and be strengthened by Your love.

Helplessness

Some wandered in desert
    wastelands,
    finding no way to a city
      where they could settle.
They were hungry and
    thirsty,
    and their lives ebbed away.
Then they cried out to the
    Lord in their trouble,
    and he delivered them
      from their distress.

(PSALM 107:4–6*)

I will lead the blind by ways
    they have not known,
    along unfamiliar paths I
      will guide them;
I will turn the darkness into
    light before them
    and make the rough places
      smooth.
These are the things I will
    do;
    I will not forsake them.

(ISAIAH 42:16*)

You feel helpless. What you're facing now seems so much bigger than you, and you don't think that you can do anything at all. You're looking for a Superman to come and save the day.

The truth is, there *are* some things you can't handle alone. But no man—super or not—will be able to help you. No, there are some things that won't be subdued by mere mortal hands. When you are confronted by such a situation, call on God. He will come to your aid. He will lift you up. He will be your superhero.

YOUR VOW TO GOD . . .

I am never helpless because I always have the power to call on You, my Lord. I will never despair, for I know that all I have to do is call and You are there.

Hopelessness

Let us hold unswervingly to the hope we profess, for he who promised is faithful.

(HEBREWS 10:23*)

Find rest, O my soul, in God
    alone;
  my hope comes from him.
He alone is my rock and my
    salvation;
  he is my fortress, I will not
    be shaken.

(PSALM 62:5–6*)

"Blessed *is* the man who trusts in the
    Lord,
And whose hope is the Lord.
For he shall be like a tree planted by the
    waters,
Which spreads out its roots by the river,
And will not fear when heat comes;
But its leaf will be green,
And will not be anxious in the year of
    drought,
Nor will cease from yielding fruit."

(JEREMIAH 17:7–8)

The paradox of hopelessness is that it does not mean you have no hope; rather, it means you have placed your hope in the wrong thing. You're too scared to hope for anything because you are so tired of being disappointed. You believe in impossibility, rather than in the one thing you should believe in—the all good, Almighty Lord.

Stop putting your trust in the limited and start trusting in Omnipotent God. Be assured that all things are possible through Him. God is the only promise that is eternally kept. Where there is God, there is hope.

YOUR VOW TO GOD . . .

I believe in You and I have faith in your steadfast promises. My hope springs eternal and I walk forward knowing that through You, the best is yet to come.

Hurt

"And I will make you to this people a
    fortified bronze wall;
And they will fight against you,
But they shall not prevail against you;
For I *am* with you to save you
And deliver you," says the Lord.
"I will deliver you from the hand of the
    wicked,
And I will redeem you from the grip of the
    terrible."

           (JEREMIAH 15:20–21)

As for me, I will call upon God,
And the Lord shall save me.
Evening and morning and at noon
I will pray, and cry aloud,
And He shall hear my voice.

           (PSALM 55:16–17)

The Lord will rescue me from every evil attack and will bring
me safely to his heavenly kingdom. To him be glory for ever
and ever. Amen.

           (2 TIMOTHY 4:18*)

Oh dear lady, I hear you crying. Someone has done you wrong. Like a fine porcelain doll someone has smashed to the floor, you are shattered. Who will mend you? Some may try, but your broken pieces are jagged and their sharp edges cut those who get too close.

But there is One who can fix you. God can mend your broken spirit. He will carefully pick up each piece and put you back together, making you whole, making you new again. The Lord Jesus Christ will restore you. The Holy Spirit will fill you up so you can never be broken again.

Your vow to God . . .

Although I am hurt and broken, I am not permanently damaged. I turn to You now and cry out and You are here. You will restore me and for that I sing Your praise.

Ignorance

[A]nd if you call out for
insight
and cry aloud for
understanding,
and if you look for it as
silver
and search for it as for
hidden treasure,
then you will understand the
fear of the Lord
and find the knowledge of
God.
For the Lord gives wisdom,
and from his mouth come
knowledge and
understanding.

(PROVERBS 2:3–6*)

For God, who said, "Let light shine out of darkness," made his light shine in our hearts to give us the light of the knowledge of the glory of God in the face of Christ.

(2 CORINTHIANS 4:6*)

Then Jesus spoke to them again, saying, "I am the light of the world. He who follows Me shall not walk in darkness, but have the light of life."

(JOHN 8:12)

I walked into a bookstore the other day and was overwhelmed by the number of titles that filled the shelves. Each volume contained a wealth of information, and I sadly acknowledged that even though I am an avid reader, I would never have the time to read them all. There were just too many books.

But then I remembered there is only one Book, and it holds the key to true wisdom. God's Word is the light that can bring you out of darkness. Embrace it and let it shine in your heart. Let Jesus be your Teacher; He will deliver you from the imprisonment of ignorance to the empowerment of knowledge. A wise woman knows she will never walk in ignorance when God is by her side.

YOUR VOW TO GOD . . .

You've granted me the wisdom to know what I don't know, and the knowledge that all I need to do is turn to You and You will teach me. I call on You now and look to Your Word so that I may be delivered from my ignorance.

Illness

Is anyone among you sick? Let him call for the elders of the church, and let them pray over him, anointing him with oil in the name of the Lord.

And the prayer of faith will save the sick, and the Lord will raise him up. And if he has committed sins, he will be forgiven.

(JAMES 5:14–15)

Therefore, since Christ suffered in his body, arm yourselves also with the same attitude, because he who has suffered in his body is done with sin. As a result, he does not live the rest of his earthly life for evil human desires, but rather for the will of God.

(1 PETER 4:1–2*)

"See to it, then, that the light within you is not darkness. Therefore, if your whole body is full of light, and no part of it dark, it will be completely lighted, as when the light of a lamp shines on you."

(LUKE 11:35–36*)

You're in so much pain and you don't know why. You've cried until the tears have run dry and asked, "Why?" so often that your voice has become hoarse. You don't understand why someone must suffer the ravages of illness.

Have faith. Somewhere down the road you will find the answer to your question. Although you may not see it now, down the road you will find Mighty Hands that hold the answers in them. Until then, recall Jesus' suffering. He cried, He bled, He died for us. In doing so, He gave us the gift of eternal life. Turn to Him and you will live forever. The body may be sick, but the soul will be healthy when the Holy Spirit fills your heart.

YOUR VOW TO GOD . . .

Instead of asking why, I will focus my energy on getting well. But even more important than that, I will find peace in the truth that through You I have eternal life.

Immorality

"If you repent, I will restore
     you that you may serve me;
if you utter worthy, not
          worthless, words,
     you will be my spokesman.
Let this people turn to you,
     but you must not turn to
          them."

(JEREMIAH 15:19B*)

Good and upright is the
          Lord;
     therefore he instructs
          sinners in his ways.
He guides the humble in
          what is right
     and teaches them his way.
All the ways of the Lord are
          loving and faithful
     for those who keep the
          demands of his covenant.

(PSALM 25:8–10*)

The unfailing love of the Lord never ends! By his mercies we
have been kept from complete destruction. Great is his faithfulness; his mercies begin afresh each day.

(LAMENTATIONS 3:22–23⁺)

Right now you feel ashamed. You look in the mirror with disgust and call yourself hundreds of different names—none of them pretty. The last thing you would think to call yourself right now is a lady. But you are a lady—you're God's lady. As such, no matter what you do, if you look to Him, He will take you in His arms and forgive you of your sins. If you ask Him, He will cleanse you and make you pure.

Bow your head in repentance, but don't keep staring at the ground. Look up and look at the Lord. Look to Him, and He will show you how He wants you to act. Often when you partake in immoral behavior, you do so to please someone else. But there is only One you have to please. When you seek God's favor, all your actions will be righteous and moral.

YOUR VOW TO GOD . . .

Lord, I want to please You. In all my thoughts, in all my words, in all my actions, I will seek to win Your favor. From this day forward, I will remain pure in heart and mind. I am a lady . . . I am Your lady.

Impatience

Even youths will become exhausted, and young men will give up. But those who wait on the Lord will find new strength. They will fly high on wings like eagles. They will run and not grow weary. They will walk and not faint.

(ISAIAH 40:30–31⁺)

Therefore be patient, brethren, until the coming of the Lord. See *how* the farmer waits for the precious fruit of the earth, waiting patiently for it until it receives the early and latter rain. You also be patient. Establish your hearts, for the coming of the Lord is at hand.

(JAMES 5:7–8)

Therefore I say to you, whatever things you ask when you pray, believe that you receive them, and you will have them.

(MARK 11:24)

Have you ever had to stand on line at the bank? It's something we all have to do. And inevitably, on occasion, there's been a person behind you who is huffing and puffing and tapping his foot. He's looking at his watch, sighing loudly and glaring at the tellers for moving too slowly. Why is he so impatient? He's going to get to the front of the line eventually. Or does he think he's more important than everybody else on that line and deserves immediate attention?

Why are *you* so impatient? Don't you trust that you are going to get what you deserve? Don't you know the Lord will take care of you? Humbly wait for your gifts and you will receive them. Trust in God's plan. Stop looking at your watch—God is always on time.

I know that everything happens when it is supposed to happen. I have faith in Your plan. I will wait on You my Lord, and I know You will reward my patience.

Indecisiveness

Now a man came up to Jesus and asked, "Teacher, what good thing must I do to get eternal life?"

"Why do you ask me about what is good?" Jesus replied. "There is only One who is good. If you want to enter life, obey the commandments."

(MATTHEW 19:16–17*)

But when he, the Spirit of truth, comes, he will guide you into all truth. He will not speak on his own; he will speak only what he hears, and he will tell you what is yet to come. He will bring glory to me by taking from what is mine and making it known to you.

(JOHN 16:13–14*)

I will praise the Lord, who
    counsels me;
  even at night my heart
    instructs me.
I have set the Lord always
    before me.
  Because he is at my right hand,
  I will not be shaken.

(PSALM 16:7–8*)

If you've ever had the television on late at night, you've undoubtedly seen a commercial for one of those psychic hot lines. People call in and pay their hard-earned money to have some charlatan tell them how to lead their lives—what to do, what job to take, who to marry. I don't understand it.

You don't need anyone to make your decisions for you. You know the answers. You have a guide. You have God. If you're feeling indecisive, if you're not trusting yourself, then you're not trusting God. He will lead you, just ask Him. Pray, read the Bible and listen to your heart. Let the Lord lead you. If you choose God you will always make the right choice.

Your vow to God . . .

Dear God, I am faced with decisions every day. But I know that if I turn to You, You will help me make the right choices. I promise to trust You, so that I can trust myself.

ndifference

I am the one who corrects and disciplines everyone I love. Be diligent and turn from your indifference.

(REVELATION 3:19+)

Enter his gates with
    thanksgiving
and his courts with praise;
give thanks to him and
    praise his name.
For the Lord is good and
    his love endures forever;
his faithfulness continues
    through all generations.

(PSALM 100:4–5*)

Do you know that you are the temple of God and that the spirit of God dwells in you?

For the temple of God is holy, which temple you are.

(1 CORINTHIANS 3:16–17B)

What sad event of yesterday, what terrible scar, keeps you from caring? Was there a time when dreams lived inside you? Didn't hope once fill your heart? I know that disappointment is painful, and you want to protect yourself from its cruel sting. You think that if you don't care you can't get hurt.

Well, when you harden your heart you may not feel the pain, but you're not feeling anything else either. Is that the way you want to live?

Invite the Lord into your heart. Let His love be the balm that softens the scars and soothes your wounds. Let His compassion fill you up and be a gift that you share with others. Know that God values and cares for you. Now you must value and care for yourself.

Your vow to God . . .

From now on I will shout, "I do care!" You value me, so I value myself. You have graced me with Your love so I must be worth it. Your gentle touch melts away the fortress I built around my heart, and with trust in You I dare to care.

Inferiority

So do not throw away your confidence; it will be richly rewarded. You need to persevere so that when you have done the will of God, you will receive what he has promised.

(HEBREWS 10:35–36*)

"I have been crucified with Christ; it is no longer I who live, but Christ lives in me; and the *life* which I now live in the flesh I live by faith in the Son of God, who loved me and gave Himself for me."

(GALATIANS 2:20)

I will praise You, for I am fearfully *and* wonderfully made. Marvelous are Your works; and that my soul knows very well.

(PSALM 139:14)

You think you should be thinner, smarter, better. You think you should be anything but what you are. And when you look around, all you can see is that everyone else seems happier, smarter, richer than you. It's like they all know the secret to life and you don't.

When you lack belief in yourself, you are lacking belief in God. But you are perfect in the eyes of He who made you. He is the author of your soul. Would He ever write anything less than a masterpiece? The Lord is an artist and you are His finest creation. Recognize His brilliance and celebrate yourself.

YOUR VOW TO GOD . . .

Lord, You are the Master Creator and I am Your work of art. I acknowledge Your magnificence in me and I humbly praise the fine work You have done.

Insecurity

Trust in the Lord with all your heart; do not depend on your own understanding. Seek his will in all you do, and he will direct your paths.

(PROVERBS 3:5–6[+])

"The kingdom of God does not come with observation; nor will they say, 'See here! or See there!' For indeed, the kingdom of God is within you."

(LUKE 17:20B–21)

"Therefore do not fear them. For there is nothing covered that will not be revealed, and hidden that will not be known.

Whatever I tell you in the dark, speak in the light; and what you hear in the ear, preach on the housetops."

(MATTHEW 10:26–27)

The high-powered executive in her dress-for-success business suit. The rich society lady in her diamonds and fur. The "super mom" who carpools, PTAs, raises kids and runs a house. They all seem to be so "together." But if you'll look closer, you'll see the trembling little girl behind their eyes—doubting, uncertain and scared.

They're just like you.

Why are you so insecure? It may be that you've been banged, bruised and beaten by cruel words, broken promises and clenched fists. It may be that everyone around you thought so little of you that you started thinking little about yourself.

But there is someone who always has faith in you and your abilities. God gave you all the tools you need to succeed. He has equipped you. He knows you are a woman of excellence. He will keep your steps steady and your position strong. Move ahead with confidence and the Lord will cheer you on.

YOUR VOW TO GOD . . .

From this day forward, I will walk my journey with confidence because I know You walk beside me. You have graced me with the gifts I need to succeed. I have faith in my abilities because I have faith in You.

Intolerance

You, therefore, have no excuse, you who pass judgment on someone else, for at whatever point you judge the other, you are condemning yourself, because you who pass judgment do the same things.

(Romans 2:1*)

My dear brothers and sisters, how can you claim that you have faith in our glorious Lord Jesus Christ if you favor some people more than others?

For instance, suppose someone comes into your meeting dressed in fancy clothes and expensive jewelry, and another comes in who is poor and dressed in shabby clothes. If you give special attention and a good seat to the rich person, but you say to the poor one, "You can stand over there, or else sit on the floor"—well, doesn't this discrimination show that you are guided by the wrong motives?...

Yes indeed, it is good when you truly obey our Lord's royal command found in the Scriptures: "Love your neighbor as yourself." But if you pay special attention to the rich, you are committing a sin, for you are guilty of breaking that law.

And the person who keeps all the laws except one is as guilty as the person who has broken all of God's laws.

(James 2:1–4, 8–10+)

It's all around you, so why not join in? Coworkers talking about how bad the boss treats you all. That delicious piece of gossip about a mutual friend. A cutting remark about how the woman across the room is dressed.

Those little bites are vicious and not appropriate for the lady God wants you to be. He wants you to lift up others, not tear them down. He wants you to build, not destroy.

Take heed and take heart. The next time you are tempted to be intolerant, just shout, *Stop!* within your mind. Remind yourself that you've just made a decision for God and that He is very pleased.

Your vow to God . . .

I am an instrument of God's peace, not a tool for the devil's pain. I will lift up my neighbor unto You, and I will remember to love them as children of God. All people are my brothers and sisters in the family of Christ.

Jealousy

[F]or you are still controlled by your own sinful desires. You are jealous of one another and quarrel with each other. Doesn't that prove you are controlled by your own desires? You are acting like people who don't belong to the Lord.

(1 CORINTHIANS 3:3⁺)

For wherever there is jealousy and selfish ambition, there you will find disorder and every kind of evil.

But the wisdom that comes from heaven is first of all pure. It is also peace loving, gentle at all times, and willing to yield to others. It is full of mercy and good deeds. It shows no partiality and is always sincere. And those who are peacemakers will plant seeds of peace and reap a harvest of goodness.

(JAMES 3:16–18⁺)

You watch as your man notices that pretty young woman who just entered the restaurant. Immediately you feel the tentacles of fear grip your mind and you have fallen victim to the sin of jealousy. Jealousy is a sin because it keeps you from loving everything that the Father has given you.

I want you to remember that your life is in His hands, and His eye never leaves you. With the Lord you can gently release your jealous thoughts and replace them with the truth of Jesus' peace. You'll feel better knowing you've just made room for His blessing to move into your life.

YOUR VOW TO GOD . . .

The Lord is my Shepherd and I shall not want. I release all thought of jealousy and instead revel in the knowledge that the gaze of the Lord is on me always. The love of Jesus satisfies me completely.

Judgment

"So whenever you speak, or whatever you do, remember that you will be judged by the law of love, the law that set you free. For there will be no mercy for you if you have not been merciful to others. But if you have been merciful, then God's mercy toward you will win out over his judgment against you."

(JAMES 2:12–13[+])

But the Lord said to Samuel, "Don't judge by his appearance or height, for I have rejected him. The Lord doesn't make decisions the way you do! People judge by outward appearance, but the Lord looks at a person's thoughts and intentions."

(1 SAMUEL 16:7[+])

"Therefore be merciful, just as your Father also is merciful.

"Judge not, and you shall not be judged. Condemn not, and you shall not be condemned. Forgive, and you will be forgiven."

(LUKE 6:36–37)

Your thoughts are as intricate as fine lace. You weave together patterns that can be beautiful and adorn your life as a godly woman. But harsh judgments stain this lace, and there is only one way to remove the stains. You must allow the blood of Jesus to wash your mind and to cleanse your heart. His love will take you from pain to purity, from judgment to joy. Isn't it wonderful to know you can give up those judgments that have bogged you down?

I know, too, that you are probably the harshest judge of one person—you. If you confess to the Lord, He will forgive you. When He forgives you, you can forgive yourself, and that fine lace will be more beautiful and pure than ever.

YOUR VOW TO GOD . . .

My heart is not proud when my mind sits in judgment. I thankfully dissolve my judgments against others and against myself, and I keep my eyes on Your light.

*L*ack of Direction

These things I have written to you who believe in the name of the Son of God, that you may know that you have eternal life, and that you may *continue* to believe in the name of the Son of God.

Now this is the confidence that we have in Him, that if we ask anything according to His will, He hears us.

(1 JOHN 5:13–14)

The Lord *is* my shepherd;
I shall not want.
He makes me to lie down in green
    pastures;
He leads me beside the still waters.
He restores my soul;
He leads me in the path of righteousness
For His name's sake.

(PSALM 23:1–3)

"For I know the plans I have for you," declares the Lord, "plans to prosper you and not to harm you, plans to give you hope and a future. Then you will call upon me and come pray to me, and I will listen to you. You will seek me and find me when you seek me with all your heart. I will be found by you."

(JEREMIAH 29:11–14*)

Don't you wish life came with a map to point you onward down the path? You could follow along and always know where you've been, where you are and where you are going. You would have direction and would never go astray.

Good news! There is a map—it is God's Word. He has promised you that He is walking beside you, guiding you to fulfill His glorious purpose. He will lead you, keeping you on track. God's map for you is revealed every day in every way. It's up to you to see it.

YOUR VOW TO GOD . . .

I see Your guiding hand everywhere I look. I can feel You fill me with Your purpose and trust that You will reveal everything I need to know. You are my compass, and Your Word is my map.

Laziness

Lazy hands make a man
>   poor,
>   but diligent hands bring
>   wealth.

(PROVERBS 10:4*)

So I perceived that nothing is better than that a man should rejoice in his own works, for that is his heritage.

(ECCLESIASTES 3:22A)

"You shall walk after the Lord your God and fear Him, and keep His commandments and obey His voice; you shall serve Him and hold fast to Him."

(DEUTERONOMY 13:4)

The reward for going to the gym every day is a healthy, attractive body. At first our muscles hurt and ache, but eventually they become toned and strong. It takes work, but it is worth it.

So it is with your heart, your mind and your soul. You must use your mental gym to exercise your spririt so that you are strong in everything that God will ask of you. Develop those godly muscles so that your strength will glorify God. Take a step every day to move forward in every area of your life, and you will move from a lazy life to a lavish one.

Your vow to God . . .

I will finally tell the truth: My soul is thirsty for You, my Lord. I look to You today to be my strength. Your love is better than life itself. I can do all things, but only through You who have saved me. Today I take a step for God.

Lies

"You shall not bear false witness against
  your neighbor."

(EXODUS 20:16)

We all make many mistakes, but those who control their tongues
can also control themselves in every other way.

(JAMES 3:2+)

Jesus told him, "I am the way, the truth, and the life. No one
can come to the Father except through me."

(JOHN 14:6+)

A lie, no matter how big or small, is a defilement against God. Sometimes you think that "a little one won't hurt anyone," but it does. It weakens your resolve and puts a barrier between you and God.

Why not begin a ministry of truth? By making truth your compass, you will always head in the right direction. You've heard the phrase "the truth will set you free." I challenge you to think about what this really means for you and how you can use this as the foundation for your life. The truth is precious—don't settle for anything else.

YOUR VOW TO GOD . . .

I hold steadfast in the truth. There is power in Your word and I believe You. I now create a life of belief, of truth and of glory to God.

*L*oneliness

"Are not two sparrows sold for a copper coin? And not one of them falls to the ground apart from your Father's will.

"But the very hairs of your head are all numbered.

"Do not fear therefore; you are of more value than many sparrows."

(MATTHEW 10:29–31)

"Look! Here I stand at the door and knock. If you hear me calling and open the door, I will come in, and we will share a meal as friends."

(REVELATION 3:20+)

He shall call upon Me, and I will answer him;
I will be with him in trouble;
I will deliver him and honor him

(PSALMS 91:15)

So much loneliness in your life. It causes you to be depressed, to believe that no one loves you, that no one could love you. "Alone is not so bad," you say, but inside you fear that you might be alone forever. You feel helpless, even desperate. The river of your loneliness gets deeper and wider until you are drowning under its current.

But you are not hidden from God. He sees you. His mighty touch brings you to safety, and His love breaks right through to that heart you thought you had guarded so well. In this one moment you can go from loneliness to love—just let Him in.

YOUR VOW TO GOD . . .

I have felt so alone, but that is only because I forgot that You are right here with me. You knew me at the beginning and You'll be with me for eternity. I will not be lonely because with You I am never alone.

Longing

And I pray that Christ will be more and more at home in your hearts as you trust in him. May your roots go down deep into the soil of God's marvelous love. And may you have the power to understand, as all God's people should, how wide, how long, how high, and how deep his love really is.

(EPHESIANS 3:17–18+)

This is real love. It is not that we loved God, but that he loved us and sent his Son as a sacrifice to take away our sins.

(1 JOHN 4:10+)

"And so I tell you, keep on asking, and you will be given what you ask for. Keep on looking, and you will find. Keep on knocking, and the door will be opened. For everyone who asks, receives. Everyone who seeks, finds. And the door is opened to everyone who knocks."

(LUKE 11:9–10+)

Have you ever wanted something so badly that you would pretty much do anything to get it? Perhaps a relationship, material goods or even just a change in your life. Whatever the situation, you long for something that you believe will fulfill you. You've become so focused on this longing that you've lost sight of everything else.

But God longs for you, for your entire heart. He wants you to submit everything to Him so He can cherish you and show you what true love really is. You can believe this: He has already given everything to you. It's now your mission to accept it. When you do, you will never long for anything again.

I cannot get from someone or something else what I can only get from You. So today I will know that You give me exactly what I need in order to be Your lady.

Loss

And I am convinced that nothing can ever separate us from his love. Death can't, and life can't. The angels can't, and the demons can't. Our fears for today, our worries about tomorrow, and even the powers of hell can't keep God's love away. Whether we are high above the sky or in the deepest ocean, nothing in all creation will ever be able to separate us from the love of God that is revealed in Christ Jesus our Lord.

(ROMANS 8:38–39⁺)

Even when I walk
    through the dark valley of death,
I will not be afraid,
    for you are close beside me.
Your rod and your staff
    protect and comfort me.

(PSALM 23:4⁺)

But in my distress I cried out to the Lord;
    yes, I prayed to my God for help.
He heard me from his sanctuary;
    my cry reached his ears.

(PSALM 18:6⁺)

What you once had is now gone, and its absence feels like raw pain. It hurts and it feels like the hurt will never go away. The pain feels like night in your soul. How much can you take?

Sometimes it's when you feel the most brokenhearted that you can hear God's voice most clearly. The walls you have spent years building have shattered and God can finally come into your heart. Ask Him right now. Ask Him to comfort you, to bring you peace. Ask Him to stay with you and give you wisdom. He's here now with you. He can heal your soul.

Your vow to God . . .

God, I hurt so much it's like my heart is on fire. Bring Your soothing water to my soul. Heal me, help me, hold me. I can make it through because You are here. Thank You for being here.

O Lord, You have searched me and know
    me.
You know my sitting down and my rising
    up;
You understand my thought afar off.
You comprehend my path and my lying
    down.
And are acquainted with all my ways.
For *there is* not a word on my tongue.
But behold, O Lord, You know it
    altogether.

(PSALM 139:1–4)

Set a guard over my mouth,
        O Lord;
    keep watch over the door
        of my lips.
Let not my heart be drawn
        to what is evil.

(PSALM 141:3–4A*)

Beloved, if God so loved us, we also ought to love one another.
(1 JOHN 4:11)

In the beginning was the Word, but sometimes words hurt. You've said things in anger or ignorance that have put a wall of fire between you and someone else. Or perhaps someone was cruel and thoughtless, verbally attacking you. Whatever the specifics, the effect is the same: You find yourself involved in a war of words.

This may sound crazy, but I want you to take miscommunication and thank God for it! Whether you realize it or not, you have been given a chance to grow even closer to someone using communication as the tool. Through your misunderstanding can come *understanding*. Through the flames can come friendship. Do not delay—ask God to soften your heart and the heart of everyone else involved. Speak and hear with your heart and let the words carry God's love.

Your vow to God . . .

God, You are the Prince of Peace, and I ask You to infuse this situation with the perfect peace You offer. I don't want this to continue. I am ready to do as You ask and to be an instrument of Your love.

Misfortune

These trials are only to test your faith, to show that it is strong and pure. It is being tested as fire tests and purifies gold—and your faith is far more precious to God than mere gold. So if your faith remains strong after being tried by fiery trials, it will bring you much praise and glory and honor on the day when Jesus Christ is revealed to the whole world.

(1 PETER 1:7+)

"For I know the plans I have for you," says the Lord. "They are plans for good and not for disaster, to give you a future and a hope."

(JEREMIAH 29:11+)

> Be not afraid, O wild animals,
>   for the open pastures are
>   becoming green.
> The trees are bearing their fruit;
>   the fig tree and the vine
>   yield their riches.
> Be glad, O people of Zion,
>   rejoice in the Lord your God,
>   for he has given you
>   a teacher for
>   righteousness.
> He sends you abundant showers,
>   both autumn and
>   spring rains, as before.

(JOEL 2:22–23*)

Winter comes at the same time every year. Cold winds bring freezing snow, and soon the landscape is blanketed in layers of ice. It gets dark earlier and earlier, until there are just a few hours of daylight each day. Are you in a winter in your life? Does it seem like misfortune is everywhere you look? Answers can be hard to find, and even guidance seems to be missing.

Hold on! Spring is coming! Stay patient and know beyond any doubt that God will take care of you. He has proven time and again how faithful He is, and like the Spring that comes every year, He will come to restore you.

YOUR VOW TO GOD . . .

God, help me to know that this misfortune in my life is temporary, but Your love is permanent. I'm willing to be patient as You shape me and bring Spring into my heart. I am Your lady and I trust You.

Need

For he will deliver the needy
who cry out,
the afflicted who have no
one to help.
He will take pity on the
weak and the needy
and save the needy from
death.

(PSALM 72:12–13*)

For the wages of sin is death, but the free gift of God is eternal life through Jesus Christ our Lord.

(ROMANS 6:23+)

Jesus replied, "If you only knew the gift God has for you and who I am, you would ask me, and I would give you living water."

(JOHN 4:10+)

What do you really need in your life? Do you have needs that are not being met? You might feel that if only you had more of this or less of that, your life would improve.

It's so easy to be hypnotized by the things you think you need that you can forget that God either gives you everything you need or gives you the tools to get it yourself. He always takes care of you, but are you accepting what He is giving? Sometimes we want what isn't best for us and reject His gifts. Through obedience to His word and trust in His guidance, you can move from need to knowing that God truly is your Provider. Put Him at the top of your list of needs and you'll need nothing else.

YOUR VOW TO GOD . . .

I've spent so much time wanting more and more, but so little time listening to Your guidance. I trust You, and I know that I can use what You give me to bring me closer to You. I now know that You are all I truly need. Thank You for everything.

egativity

What is faith? It is the confident assurance that what we hope for is going to happen. It is the evidence of things we cannot yet see.

(HEBREWS 11:1[+])

Those who are dominated by the sinful nature think about sinful things, but those who are controlled by the Holy Spirit think about things that please the Spirit. If your sinful nature controls your mind, there is death. But if the Holy Spirit controls your mind, there is life and peace.

(ROMANS 8:5–6[+])

His brilliant splendor fills the heavens, and the earth is filled with his praise! What a wonderful God he is! Rays of brilliant light flash from his hands. He rejoices in his awesome power.

(HABAKKUK 3:3B–4[+])

Beware of the life-suckers! These creatures walk the earth sapping you of your joy of life. Oh, these guys are dangerous. They are so subtle. One negative comment is all it takes to infect you, and like the flu it will begin to break you down. Let one negative thought into your brain and soon you will be viewing all of life with negative eyes.

If you're feeling negative right now, invite Christ into your life. We are told that when we are alive with Jesus, we will see through new eyes. Ask the Lord, and He will help you see all the wonderful things right in front of you. Pray to the Holy Spirit to guard you from negativity. Let the Spirit crush the life-suckers before they crush you.

Your vow to God . . .

When negativity threatens to overtake me, I will look to You, my Lord. Help me see all the positive things in my life and protect me from those who try to infect me. I will keep You in my heart so that I may be immune from other people's negative attitudes.

eglect

Dearest friends, you were always so careful to follow my instructions when I was with you. And now that I am away you must be even more careful to put into action God's saving work in your lives, obeying God with deep reverence and fear. For God is working in you, giving you the desire to obey him and the power to do what pleases him.

(PHILIPPIANS 2:12–13[+])

Do not neglect the spiritual gift you received through the prophecies spoken to you when the elders of the church laid their hands on you. Give your complete attention to these matters. Throw yourself into your tasks so that everyone will see your progress. Keep a close watch on yourself and on your teaching. Stay true to what is right, and God will save you and those who hear you.

(1 TIMOTHY 4:14–16[+])

And we know that God causes everything to work together for the good of those who love God and are called according to his purpose for them.

(ROMANS 8:28[+])

I don't know if you've ever had a garden, but they require a lot of work. Besides preparing the soil and planting the seeds, you must remember to water it and pull out any weeds. If you neglect it for even a little while, the plants might wither and die.

So it is with your life. If others are neglecting you, maybe it's time you became your own gardener. God has planted the seeds of greatness within you. Water yourself with compassion and pull the weeds of doubt, negativity or despair. One excellent way to do this is by using daily prayer and the reading of God's Word. By taking time each day to nourish yourself and your relationship with God, you will reap a great harvest and cultivate beautiful flowers in your soul.

Your vow to God . . .

Starting today I will take time each and every day to pray, praise and prepare myself for Your will. I won't neglect the seeds You have carefully and lovingly planted. When I care for myself I honor You. I will cultivate Your garden and flourish in the light of Your love.

besity

But food does not commend us to God.

(1 CORINTHIANS 8:8A)

Again Jesus called the crowd to him and said, "Listen to me, everyone, and understand this. Nothing outside a man can make him 'unclean' by going into him. Rather, it is what comes out of a man that makes him 'unclean.'"

(MARK 7:14–15*)

But if I partake with thanks, why am I evil spoken of for *the food* over which I give thanks?

Therefore, whether you eat or drink, or whatever you do, do all to the glory of God.

(1 CORINTHIANS 10:30–31)

You've dieted, starved yourself, walked miles on the treadmill and tried to lose weight through pills, powders and prayer. You wrestle with yourself, believing that if you looked a certain way, then you would be more acceptable in the eyes of the world, more beautiful to men and more lovable to yourself.

You've left someone out of the equation. The Lord has an image of the perfect woman—you! He created you in His image, and is extremely pleased. He does want you to lose something though: your old self-image. Move from less calories to more confidence, from low-fat to high-praise. You are no less than the beloved daughter of the Heavenly Father, and He loves who you are and who you are becoming.

Your vow to God . . .

No more starving, no more self-hatred. Today I begin by loving my body as a gift from God. I ask the Holy Spirit to guard me from everything that would defile His temple, and to give me strength, confidence and poise.

Oppression

The Lord is a refuge for the
  oppressed,
  a stronghold in times of
  trouble.
Those who know your name
  will trust in you,
  for you, Lord, have never
  forsaken those who seek
  you

(PSALM 9:9–10*)

[B]ut he gives us more grace?
That is why Scripture says:
  "God opposes the proud
  but gives grace to the
  humble."

(JAMES 4:6*)

I lay down and slept;
I awoke, for the Lord sustained me.
I will be not afraid of ten thousands of people
who have set themselves against me all around.

(PSALM 3:5–6)

You feel like you are being attacked from all directions. You're being held back, held down. You're being held in a tiny little box, and someone is sitting on the lid. You want out, you need help. But who can you trust? Who can help?

The Lord is more powerful than anyone or anything. He is always ready to help you. Jesus is the Lord of freedom. He looses the chains of oppression and throws them away. He is the great Emancipator, and leads His people out of slavery. There is only One way to freedom, and it's through Jesus Christ.

Your vow to God . . .

O Lord, help me to get out of the oppression I am experiencing. Where you lead, I will follow. I can do all things through You who lives in me, and through Your strength I will overcome everything and everyone who tries to oppress me.

Overwhelmed

Whatever you do, work at it with all your heart, as working for the Lord, not for men, since you know that you will receive an inheritance from the Lord as a reward. It is the Lord Christ you are serving. Anyone who does wrong will be repaid for his wrong, and there is no favoritism.

(COLOSSIANS 3:23–24*)

For this is the love of God, that we keep His commandments. And His commandments are not burdensome.

For whatever is born of God overcomes the world. And this is the victory that has overcome the world—our faith.

(1 JOHN 5:3–4)

Give your burdens to the Lord,
and he will take care of you.
He will not permit the godly to slip and fall.
(PSALM 55:22+)

There is so much that can overwhelm you. Stress at work, the kids, your marriage, bills and even the car needs repair. Dinner needs to be made, errands need to be run and you've got to take care of every other little thing. It's easy to feel overrun, overextended and, yes, overwhelmed. You might even feel like you're at the breaking point. You're doing so much and yet there's even more to do.

Turn your attention, even for a second, to the sacrifices that Jesus made to give you life. Once you realize how deeply He cares for you, you'll be overwhelmed—this time by the love of Christ for you. With this new focus, you'll be able to prioritize the rest of your life. Start with Jesus and you'll never end up with more than you can handle.

Your vow to God . . .

I take a deep breath and feel the lift You have given me. This is the day You have made, and I live it gratefully. Starting here and now I place You at the top of my priorities. I just do my best, knowing You will do for me what I cannot do for myself.

Pain

Always be joyful. Keep on praying. No matter what happens, always be thankful, for this is God's will for you who belong to Christ Jesus.

(1 Thessalonians 5:16–18[+])

"I command you—be strong and courageous! Do not be afraid or discouraged. For the Lord your God is with you wherever you go."

(Joshua 1:9[+])

The Lord himself watches over you!
   The Lord stands beside you as your protective
      shade.
The sun will not hurt you by day,
   nor the moon at night.
The Lord keeps you from all evil
   and preserves your life.
The Lord keeps watch over you as you come and
      go,
   both now and forever.

(Psalm 121:5–8[+])

Whether your pain is physical, emotional or spiritual, the one constant is: It hurts. Pain takes over and creates a bleeding spirit. Your pain is so bad sometimes that you cry out to the Lord, "Help me! Help me!"

God hears your cries, and He is here with you right now. He aches *with* you and aches *for* you. Jesus is the God of healing and hope. When you can barely move forward, He is there, walking with you, holding you. He is the relief to a life of pain, and is leading you to His healing tonic of love.

Your vow to God . . .

I will love You today more than I feel my pain. I choose to thrive, not just survive. Pain is not my master. You, Jesus, are my Master. And today I will serve You.

Panic

It is better to be patient than powerful; it is better to have self-control than to conquer a city.

(PROVERBS 16:32⁺)

Be glad for all God is planning for you. Be patient in trouble, and always be prayerful.

(ROMANS 12:12⁺)

And now, all glory to God, who is able to keep you from stumbling, and who will bring you into his glorious presence innocent of sin and with great joy. All glory to him, who alone is God our Savior, through Jesus Christ our Lord. Yes, glory, majesty, power, and authority belong to him, in the beginning, now, and forevermore. Amen.

(JUDE 1:24–25⁺)

Panic makes you feel like a small child who is lost in a huge, busy mall—screaming for your mother, terrified that no one can find you. The fear is terrible. Your panic makes you feel that the worst that can happen is about to happen, and you are powerless to change it. You believe that you could be left alone, left behind. Can you relate to this?

God has a special promise for you. He has promised you that there is no place on earth or in your heart that you could hide where He would not find you, where He would not be there with you. Take assurance in His promises, and let them calm you. Release the grip panic has on you, and you'll find that God is in control, as He has been all along.

YOUR VOW TO GOD . . .

You are the Alpha and the Omega, and You have the whole world in the palm of Your hand. I reject the lie that I am alone and feel Your strength in me and in my life. I don't need to panic because I feel Your peace.

Persecution

"But I say to you who hear: Love your enemies, do good to those who hate you, bless those who curse you, and pray for those who spitefully use you.

"To him who strikes you on the *one* cheek, offer the other also. And from him who takes away your cloak, do not withhold your tunic either."

(LUKE 6:27–29)

If someone says, "I love God," and hates his brother, he is a liar; for he who does not love his brother whom he has seen, how can he love God whom he has not seen?"

And this commandment we have from Him: that he who loves God *must* love his brother also.

(1 JOHN 4:20–21)

It is you who gives us victory over our enemies;
    it is you who humbles those who hate us.
O God, we give glory to you all day long
    and constantly praise your name.

(PSALM 44:7–8+)

You hear the malicious whispers when you walk by. Or maybe they say mean things right to your face. You're being picked on and picked apart, the victim of ugly gossip and cruel names. Why do they persecute you? Jealousy? Or are they intolerant of your differences and so they mock you because they don't understand your ways?

You know what? It doesn't matter. Stay true to who you are, because when you do you are staying true to God. You are serving the purpose He has for you.

The Bible is filled with accounts of people who were persecuted for serving Jesus Christ. But Jesus promises us that those who suffer from persecution, and do so in His name, will be delivered from their pain. He has promised to always be on your side. Make every thought of reconciliation, and make every action honest and true to Him. You will make it through this persecution. His love will see you through.

YOUR VOW TO GOD . . .

I feel persecuted. Please be with me today and make Your presence known. I will trust You and I will meet the chaos with the grace, confidence and love that You inspire in me. I dedicate my life to You.

Pettiness

You must make allowance for each other's faults and forgive the person who offends you. Remember, the Lord forgave you, so you must forgive others.

(COLOSSIANS 3:13+)

And now I want to urge you, dear lady, that we should love one another. This is not a new commandment, but one we had from the beginning.

(2 JOHN 1:5+)

Now they are here, and they are the ones who are creating divisions among you. They live by natural instinct because they do not have God's Spirit living in them.

But you, dear friends, must continue to build your lives on the foundation of your holy faith. And continue to pray as you are directed by the Holy Spirit. Live in such a way that God's love can bless you as you wait for the eternal life that our Lord Jesus Christ in his mercy is going to give you.

(JUDE 1:19–21+)

Every little thing seems to bother you. Each annoyance is like a pebble in your shoe, cutting into your foot. At first it's a minor discomfort, but the more you walk on it, the more it hurts, until it causes a big blister. Soon you're hobbling along and it's almost too painful to walk.

Your petty concerns are like those small stones. Get rid of them before they cripple you. When you feel slighted, when you think that things aren't fair, remember that these small things don't really matter. What matters is that you keep in mind that the Lord loves you and wants you to forgive others the way He forgives you. Let the Holy Spirit direct you so that you live as the lady God wants you to be.

Your vow to God . . .

I will release the little rocks of petty concern and let Your love guide me. I know that the only important thing is that I continue to walk down the path that You have placed before me. I reach out my hand to You so that You can show me the way.

rocrastination

Yet we hear that some of you are living idle lives, refusing to work and wasting time meddling in other people's business. In the name of the Lord Jesus Christ, we appeal to such people—no, we command them: Settle down and get to work. Earn your own living. And I say to the rest of you, dear brothers and sisters, never get tired of doing good.

(2 Thessalonians 3:11–13⁺)

Do what is good and run from evil—that you may live! Then the Lord God Almighty will truly be your helper, just as you have claimed he is.

(Amos 5:14⁺)

"But I will offer sacrifices to you with songs of praise, and I will fulfill all my vows. For my salvation comes from the Lord alone."

(Jonah 2:9⁺)

You've been putting things off again. What is it this time? Your dentist appointment? Balancing the check-book? Or is it the project at work that you know is going to take more than a little overtime? You procrastinate when you're faced with an unpleasant task, putting off for tomorrow what you can't bear to do today.

If you think about it, all those tasks, although unpleasant at first, will ultimately benefit you. Isn't this a lot like life in general? Sometimes it is so, so hard. But we persevere suffering like Christ but *with Christ*, so we will eventually receive our holy reward. The Apostle Paul tells us that the sufferings of this present time are not worthy *to be compared* with the glory that shall be revealed in us (Romans 8:17). He's saying that if you think about the reward, the pain it took to get it becomes insignificant.

Keep this in mind as you look over your to-do list, and if you're faced with an unpleasant task, do it first. Focus on the end and begin right away.

Your vow to God . . .

Dear Lord, there are some things I just hate to do, but I will do them and I will do them now. I will remember that no matter what task faces me, You are with me and will see me through.

Resentment

Let all bitterness, wrath, anger, clamor, and evil speaking be put away from you, with all malice. And be kind to one another, tenderhearted, forgiving one another, even as God in Christ forgave you.

(EPHESIANS 4:31–32)

But I say to you who hear: Love your enemies, do good to those who hate you, bless those who curse you, and pray for those who spitefully use you.

(LUKE 6:27–28)

Do not let your heart envy
sinners,
but always be zealous for the
fear of the Lord.
There is surely a future
hope for you,
and your hope will not be
cut off.

(PROVERBS 23:17–18*)

Resentment eats away at you, gnaws at your mind, erodes anything positive and good. It closes your heart off until no blessings can enter. You become barren and weak, more like the walking wounded than the whole woman God intends you to be.

But there is an antidote to your resentment. Begin to appreciate every single thing in your life, all that God has blessed you with. Release the resentment that squeezes the life out of you and fill your heart with the love of Christ. He's reaching out for you right now. Take His hand, and you'll be free forever.

YOUR VOW TO GOD . . .

No longer does resentment plague my mind and heart. I release it so that You can sculpt me and make me the lady You want me to be. I love growing in Your love.

Selfishness

Don't be selfish; don't live to make a good impression on others. Be humble, thinking of others as better than yourself.

(PHILIPPIANS 2:3[+])

And so, dear brothers and sisters, I plead with you to give your bodies to God. Let them be a living and holy sacrifice—the kind he will accept. When you think of what he has done for you, is this too much to ask?

(ROMANS 12:1[+])

"And whoever exalts himself will be humbled, and he who humbles himself will be exalted."

(MATTHEW 23:12)

There have been bestselling books on the art of self-ishness—isn't that amazing? There are books that teach you how to be more and more consumed with yourself. What a waste! It's a sham, a house of cards! When the house of cards begins to fall, there is nothing left. What has selfishness brought you? Nothing!

Can I tell you what is the ultimate selfish act? It's not being exactly who God intended you to be. If you are anything less, then you are not being true to the Creator. Your life is precious to Him, and He doesn't want you to waste it on things that don't matter. What does matter, however, is to live as fully, as joyfully and as meaning-fully as possible. This is only done by living through Him. He is your Savior.

YOUR VOW TO GOD . . .

Father, I will be exactly the woman You have asked me to be. I will die to my old ways, and live anew in Your love. Your vision for me is what I now make mine. Instill in me the desires and actions that glorify and worship You, for You alone are the Holy One.

Separation

"Am I a God near at hand," says the Lord, "And not a God afar off?"

(JEREMIAH 23:23)

"What's more, I will be with you, and I will protect you wherever you go. I will someday bring you safely back to this land. I will be with you constantly until I have finished giving you everything I promised."

(GENESIS 28:15+)

There are many ways you can feel separation. Perhaps you are separated from ones you love because you live in different areas. Or maybe you are separated because of marital problems. Whatever the reason, separation can feel like you're being torn in two. The loneliness can knock the wind right out of you and sometimes it's difficult to move forward.

But take solace in the knowledge that you are never alone, because you can never be truly separated from God. Any feelings of being apart from the Lord stem from you, not Him. But you can remedy that right now by praying to Him, thanking Him for being your constant companion. Just call on Him, and you'll never be distanced from the Lord.

YOUR VOW TO GOD . . .

I am always united with those I love in my heart. God, I know You are always with me, and that I can never be separated from You. I go through the day feeling whole and complete.

Shame

Then if my people who are called by my name will humble themselves and pray and seek my face and turn from their wicked ways, I will hear from heaven and will forgive their sins and heal their land.

(2 CHRONICLES 7:14+)

And I will give you a new heart with new and right desires, and I will put a new spirit in you. I will take out your stony heart of sin and give you a new, obedient heart.

(EZEKIEL 36:26+)

For this reason, since the day we heard about you, we have not stopped praying for you and asking God to fill you with the knowledge of his will through all spiritual wisdom and under- standing. And we pray this in order that you may live a life worthy of the Lord and may please him in every way: bearing fruit in every good work, growing in the knowledge of God, being strengthened with all power according to his glorious might so that you may have great endurance and patience, and joyfully giving thanks to the Father, who has qualified you to share in the inheritance of the saints in the kingdom of light.

(COLOSSIANS 1:9–12*)

Shame can feel like walking through life carrying heavy baggage with you wherever you go. You believe that you need those heavy suitcases filled with past experiences with you all day, every day. The past can be so heavy, can't it? And the heaviness can slow you down until you've stopped. It's too hard to go on.

You might feel like the shame is so bad that you'll never feel clean again. But the Lord has promised you that He sees the purity in you. He doesn't cling to your past, He sees you as the beautiful lady He created. The past is the past. Take it to God, give Him that baggage and then walk confidently forward—lighter, happier and spotless!

Your vow to God . . .

There is nothing from my past that can withhold Your love from me. I've held onto these secrets for so long, but now I'm ready to leave the past where it belongs—in the past. With You holding my hand and my heart, I can finally live in the "now" and move joyously into my future.

Short-tempered

Since an overseer is entrusted with God's work, he must be blameless—not overbearing, not quick-tempered, not given to much wine, not violent, not pursuing dishonest gain. Rather he must be hospitable, one who loves what is good, who is self-controlled, upright, holy and disciplined. He must hold firmly to the trustworthy message as it has been taught, so that he can encourage others by sound doctrine and refute those who oppose it.

(TITUS 1:7–9*)

A patient man has great
understanding,
but a quick-tempered man
displays folly.

(PROVERBS 14:29*)

Love is patient, love is kind. It does not envy, it does not boast, it is not proud. It is not rude, it is not self-seeking, it is not easily angered, it keeps no record of wrongs.

(1 CORINTHIANS 13:4–5*)

You snapped at the kids this morning. You yelled at that person at work. You screamed at the driver in the car that nearly cut you off on the road. You fought with your man again. Perhaps you are feeling all of the pressures in your life and pouring your frustrations out on the ones you love—and anyone who crosses your path. Or perhaps your anger is the by-product of the bitterness that has invaded your soul.

The answer is not to take this all out on those around you. The answer is to ask God to move into your heart and heal you. The healing will come from the inside out, which means that first you must let God heal your heart and only then will you notice the change in the rest of your life. God is always the answer.

Your vow to God . . .

I will act in Your love, rather than react with petty anger. Instead of being short in temper I will now choose to be long in patience. Your love rules my life.

Sin

Revive me, O Lord, for Your name's sake!
For Your righteousness' sake bring my
   soul out of trouble.

(PSALM 143:11)

See to it, brothers, that none of you has a sinful, unbelieving heart that turns away from the living God. But encourage one another daily, as long as it is called Today, so that none of you may be hardened by sin's deceitfulness.

(HEBREWS 3:12–13*)

So humble yourselves before God. Resist the Devil, and he will flee from you. Draw close to God, and God will draw close to you. Wash your hands, you sinners; purify your hearts, you hypocrites.

(JAMES 4:7–8+)

Wouldn't it be great if we were given an instruction book for life, so that we knew what to do and what not to do? Good news—we were! It's the Holy Bible. God's word teaches that sin is anything that is not of Him. Sinful behavior is doing anything that God does not want you to do. What sins have you committed?

Whatever the sins, you must know that you are human, but God is perfect. Jesus died so that the sins of humanity could be forgiven and forgotten. What you must do is to admit the sin you've committed, confess those sins unto the Lord, ask for His forgiveness and then release the sin and the sinful behavior. It takes humbleness and awareness, but the reward is a clean, new life. Ultimately you'll be spending the rest of eternity with God, your Creator. How's that for a good deal?

YOUR VOW TO GOD . . .

God, I've sinned and I ask for Your forgiveness. I'm truly sorry for what I've done. Please clean my heart, my mind and my soul so that I can feel like the pure lady I want to be, that You created me to be.

Stress

Lord, my heart is not proud;
    my eyes are not haughty.
I don't concern myself with matters too great
    or awesome for me.
But I have stilled and quieted myself,
    just as a small child is quiet with its mother.
    Yes, like a small child is my soul within me.
(PSALM 131:1–2+)

"If you keep quiet at a time like this, deliverance for the Jews will arise from some other place, but you and your relatives will die. What's more, who can say but that you have been elevated to the palace for just such a time as this?"
(ESTHER 4:14+)

Call upon Me in the day of trouble;
I will deliver you, and you shall glorify me.
(PSALM 50:15)

Stress can assail you at home, at work, every day in every way. When the stress grows, you can be overwhelmed by feelings of not having enough time or resources to take care of everything. You burn out and feel so small compared to how big the stressing force looks. What do you do? Where do you start?

You are not going through your day or your life alone. God is with you, and brings His peace to you right now. Jesus promised that new life in Him will give you an eternity of peace. All you have to do is give your whole heart to the Lord, and wait patiently for Him. His timing is perfect, His mercy is endless. When you feel stressed out, cling to God.

YOUR VOW TO GOD . . .

Your peace now permeates to my very being. I will go through this day with Your strength and love. I can handle everything now that I know I am not alone.

uffering

For *it is* better, if it is the will of God, to suffer for doing good than for doing evil.

(1 PETER 3:17)

[B]ut rejoice to the extent that you partake of Christ's sufferings, that when His glory is revealed, you may also be glad with exceeding joy.

(1 PETER 4:13)

Yet what we suffer now is nothing compared to the glory he will give us later. For all creation is waiting eagerly for that future day when God will reveal who his children really are.

(ROMANS 8:18–19⁺)

There is no such thing as hopelessness. But it can feel like everything is hopeless when you are suffering. Your soul is screaming and your heart is heavy. The pain can get unbearable.

Let me repeat that no situation is hopeless once you invite the Lord to help. He is weeping for you, and He wants to comfort you. Turn to Him, rely on Him. He is the one certainty in whom you can believe. When the suffering becomes unbearable, let God bear the load. He is the God of reconciliation and healing. He will heal your soul.

Your vow to God . . .

I suffer, Lord. I know You are the King of Peace—pour out Your peace on me. Hold me close to Your heart. I turn to You in this time of need and am grateful that I can rely on You.

Unappreciated

May our Lord Jesus Christ and God our Father, who loved us and in his special favor gave us everlasting comfort and good hope, comfort your hearts and give you strength in every good thing you do and say.

(2 THESSALONIANS 2:16–17+)

Don't be afraid, for I am with you. Do not be dismayed, for I am your God. I will strengthen you. I will help you. I will uphold you with my victorious right hand.

(ISAIAH 41:10+)

You prepare a feast for me
    in the presence of my enemies.
You welcome me as a guest,
    anointing my head with oil.
    My cup overflows with blessings.
Surely your goodness and unfailing love will
        pursue me
    all the days of my life,
and I will live in the house of the Lord
    forever.

(PSALM 23:5–6+)

Thank you. Two simple words, but oh how much they are worth! Has it been a while since you heard them? You do so much for so many people, and you just want their appreciation.

Family, friends and coworkers may neglect to thank you, but know, sweet lady, that you are appreciated by your Heavenly Father for all you do and all you are. You are fulfilling His purpose everyday. You are being the daughter He created you to be. God said that He knows you so intimately that He has even counted every hair on your head! He is active in your life and loves you dearly. You are His lady and there is never even one tiny second that He forgets that. You are always adored, anointed and appreciated.

YOUR VOW TO GOD . . .

All that I do, I do for You. And I know that You appreciate me—look at all the gifts in my life that You have given me! And in return I thank You, my Lord. I praise and honor You throughout the day through my thoughts, words and actions.

Uncharitableness

Then he turned to his host. "When you put on a luncheon or a dinner," he said, "don't invite your friends, brothers, relatives, and rich neighbors. For they will repay you by inviting you back. Instead, invite the poor, the crippled, the lame, and the blind. Then at the resurrection of the godly, God will reward you for inviting those who could not repay you."

(LUKE 14:12–14+)

Keep on loving each other as brothers. Do not forget to entertain strangers, for by so doing some people have entertained angels without knowing it.

(HEBREWS 13:1–2*)

Be imitators of God, therefore, as dearly loved children and live a life of love, just as Christ loved us and gave himself up for us as a fragrant offering and sacrifice to God.

(EPHESIANS 5:1–2*)

Somewhere between greed, selfishness and resentment is an attitude that is called uncharitableness. An uncharitable spirit starts from the fear that somehow God could forsake you, that there aren't enough of His blessings to go around. Therefore you want to hoard what you have, even if it means denying others.

Jesus commanded His followers to give away everything they had and to start all over with Him. When you give, it makes room for even more blessings to enter your life. There is no end to the riches of God's spirit, and He wants you to partake fully in His abundant life. Stop hoarding, start helping—you'll be all the more blessed because of it.

YOUR VOW TO GOD . . .

I freely and fearlessly give to others in need. You have commanded me to die daily and take on Your life as my life. I give away everything because I don't want anything standing between You and me. I happily and joyously give, and I accept Your love in return.

Unforgiving

"So watch yourselves. If your brother sins, rebuke him, and if he repents, forgive him. If he sins against you seven times in a day, and seven times comes back to you and says, 'I repent,' forgive him."

(LUKE 17:3–4*)

For if you forgive men when they sin against you, your heavenly Father will also forgive you. But if you do not forgive men their sins, your Father will not forgive your sins.

(MATTHEW 6:14–15*)

"And when you stand praying, if you hold anything against anyone, forgive him, so that your Father in heaven may forgive your sins."

(MARK 11:25*)

You've been hurt so bad that you've retreated into that inner fortress where you think you'll be protected. And you don't want to forgive those who have betrayed you because the wound is still too fresh. But unforgiveness becomes a god, a grudge that you worship. It prevents you from moving forward because you are stuck in pain.

Jesus gives you His grace freely. When He died, He prayed, "Father, forgive them, for they do not know what they do" (Luke 23:34). He forgave those who persecuted Him, and has called us to forgive those who persecute us. But you won't be doing it alone—God will work through you. God who forgives you will give you the wisdom and the understanding to forgive yourself and all others.

Your vow to God . . .

Thank You for forgiving me! With Your help, I can now move from betrayal to forgiveness. I am ready to forgive anyone who hurt me, and to begin the healing process.

Ungratefulness

"But when you are invited, go and sit down in the lowest place, so that when he who invited comes he may say to you, 'Friend, go up higher.' Then you will have glory in the presence of those who sit at the table with you."

(LUKE 14:10)

You know how full of love and kindness our Lord Jesus Christ was. Though he was very rich, yet for your sakes he became poor, so that by his poverty he could make you rich.

(2 CORINTHIANS 8:9[+])

"...Assuredly, I say to you, unless you are converted and become as little children, you will by no means enter the kingdom of heaven.

"Therefore whoever humbles himself as this little child is the greatest in the kingdom of heaven."

(MATTHEW 18:3–4)

You were so excited to get that gift. With eager fingers you ripped off the paper, tore open the box, and inside was . . . the ugliest thing you'd ever seen! How dare that person think you could ever like something like that! What was she thinking?

What she was thinking was that she wanted to do something nice for you. She wanted to give you a gift. How can you turn your back on someone's kindness? Show gratitude for the gifts you are given from others and especially from the Lord. You are blessed in many ways, but when you fail to appreciate those blessings, you feel you have nothing. Thank others and thank God for all the riches in your life.

YOUR VOW TO GOD . . .

I recognize all you give me every single day, and I thank You. I will appreciate those who are in my life and the acts of kindness they bestow upon me. My Lord, please make me worthy to receive the gifts You present to me. I am grateful for the riches in my life.

Unhappiness

All Scripture is inspired by God and is useful to teach us what is true and to make us realize what is wrong in our lives. It straightens us out and teaches us to do what is right. It is God's way of preparing us in every way, fully equipped for every good thing God wants us to do.

(2 Timothy 3:16–17⁺)

"I am leaving you with a gift—peace of mind and heart. And the peace I give isn't like the peace the world gives. So don't be troubled or afraid."

(John 14:27⁺)

He turns a desert into pools of water,
and the parched ground into flowing springs.

(Psalm 107:35*)

Many ladies come to me with the cloud of unhappiness hanging over them. They feel unappreciated at work or at home. Some feel lonely, others feel unfulfilled. All of this unhappiness stems from feeling that their lives are not going as they want.

God has a plan for your life, and your life is part of His master plan. He has put you exactly where He needs you for His purpose. Don't despair, never give up. When you know that you are a vital part of His vision, then you can find meaning in everything you do. He is the reason for everything.

Your vow to God . . .

Now I remember that you created me for Your purpose. There's a meaning for my life, and I now allow the Holy Spirit to direct me. Show me everything You need me to know. Renew my life with Your joyful spirit.

Unworthiness

This letter is from Paul, a slave of God and an apostle of Jesus Christ. I have been sent to bring faith to those God has chosen and to teach them to know the truth that shows them how to live godly lives. This truth gives them the confidence of eternal life, which God promised them before the world began—and he cannot lie.

(TITUS 1:1–2+)

You will have plenty to eat,
    until you are full,
    and you will praise the
        name of the Lord your
        God,
    who has worked wonders
        for you;
    never again will my people
        be shamed.

(JOEL 2:26–27*)

The Sovereign Lord is my strength! He will make me as sure-footed as a deer and bring me safely over the mountains.

(HABAKKUK 3:19+)

Maybe you've sinned. Maybe you have done something terrible. You feel dirty and damaged, and you're ashamed of who you are. Looking around, all you see are ways that you fall short of the glory of God. You feel so small.

But there is no reason to think you're unworthy of God's love. One of the most amazing things about our Lord is that He loves us no matter what we've done. He is the God of second chances, and if you ask Him, He will forgive you. His love will wash away the filth and restore you to purity.

Your vow to God . . .

God, I've done some awful things, but I don't want to be dirty anymore. I ask for Your forgiveness and know that You will restore me. I am worthy in Your eyes. I am a woman of excellence. I am Your lady.

Vanity

You save the humble
but bring low to those whose
eyes are haughty.

(PSALM 18:27*)

Young men, in the same way be submissive to those who are older. Clothe yourselves with humility toward one another, because,

"God opposes the proud
but gives graces to the humble."

Humble yourselves, therefore, under God's mighty hand, that he may lift you up in due time.

(1 PETER 5:5–6*)

As a prisoner for the Lord, then, I urge you to live a life worthy of the calling you have received. Be completely humble and gentle; be patient, bearing with one another in love. Make every effort to keep the unity of the Spirit through the bond of peace.

(EPHESIANS 4:1–3*)

Vanity is a lady who doesn't go out without her makeup, or without every hair in the most perfect place. Vanity is a woman who wears clothes that are too tight, high heels and cares more about what others think of her than what she thinks of herself. She spends hours in front of the mirror making sure it's all put together before she gives it all away.

I'm not fooled. I know the pain that her lipstick and hairspray are masking. She believes that if she doesn't paint herself up, then others can see inside, see the pain and emptiness she feels. She has decorated her face and body, but she hasn't decorated her soul. She acts like a queen but she's really the Queen of Nothing. Secretly she wants to be loved not for the way she looks, but for who she really is. But she can't get love from other people that she can only get from God and from herself. She must turn to God, turn to the Great Redeemer to transform her soul from the inside out. Only through Him can she become the lady God has intended all along.

YOUR VOW TO GOD . . .

I am Your lady. I am adorned in the beauty of Your joy, jeweled with Your love, and made-up in Your forgiveness. I want to be a mirror for the woman You have commanded me to be. I am Your lady.

Vengefulness

Make sure that nobody pays back wrong for wrong, but always try to be kind to each other and to everyone else.

(1 THESSALONIANS 5:15*)

"'Do not seek revenge or bear a grudge against one of your people, but love your neighbor as yourself. I am the Lord.'"

(LEVITICUS 19:18*)

Do not be overcome by evil, but overcome evil with good.

(ROMANS 12:21)

Someone has done you wrong and you are out to get him. A man has left you, a coworker has stolen from you, a friend has betrayed you—and you are out for vengeance. Revenge, you think, will taste so sweet. You'll be vindicated and you'll win. But it'll be an empty victory, because you may have won the game, but you've lost your soul.

"Vengeance is mine," said the Lord, and you are to leave God's work to God. He wants you to behave as His emissary in the world, as an example of His transforming love. But how can you be an example of it unless you've been transformed by it? Let go of the plans for revenge and know that God sees all, and will take care of everything in His way. It's not for you to do. Isn't that a relief? Aren't you glad to have the burden of vengeance off your shoulders? Now you'll be able to love Him even more.

YOUR VOW TO GOD . . .

I leave to You what is Yours, and instead do the work that You've placed in front of me. I know that You have called me to be Your disciple. Please transform me through the power of the Holy Spirit so that I can live the life You've given me more fully.

eakness

[To] the weak I became as weak, that I might win the weak. I have become all things to all *men*, that I might by all means save some.

(1 CORINTHIANS 9:22)

You therefore, my son, be strong in the grace that is in Christ Jesus.

(2 TIMOTHY 2:1)

And when I was present with you, and in need, I was a burden to no one, for what I lacked the brethren who came from Macedonia supplied. And in everything I kept myself from being burdensome to you, and so I will keep *myself*.

(2 CORINTHIANS 11:9)

You're broken. You feel as if your wings have never mended fully after the fall. It's hard to go on, it's hard to do anything at all. You believe you are just one small woman up against such powerful enemies. You wonder how you can expect any kind of happy life when you are so weak. Everyone in your life seems to echo how weak you are because they are stepping all over you.

Woman, take up the mighty sword of Jesus! Take His love as your shield, His promises are your sword. You are not defenseless—don't believe those lies! You are strong in the Lord, and He will always protect His lady. He won't let you falter, He won't let you fail. You will be victorious because the battle is over already and Jesus won. Take heart, you'll persevere. God is on your side—who can be against you?

Your vow to God . . .

I no longer listen to lies about how weak or helpless I am. I throw away the lies and believe the promises that You've told me. I carry Your strength like a protective shield, and I feel victorious in Your love. You are the winner, and I'm glad to be on Your team!

Weariness

Bear one another's burdens, and so fulfill the law of Christ.

(GALATIANS 6:2)

O Israel, how can you say that the Lord does not see your troubles? How can you say God refuses to hear your case? Have you never heard or understood? Don't you know that the Lord is the everlasting God, the Creator of all the earth? He never grows faint or weary. No one can measure the depths of his understanding. He gives power to those who are tired and worn out; he offers strength to the weak.

(ISAIAH 40:27–29[+])

For I can do everything with the help of Christ who gives me the strength I need.

(PHILIPPIANS 4:13[+])

You are so weary. You've taken care of everyone in your life—everyone, that is, except for yourself. You've washed and cleaned, you've primped and planned, you've scrimped and saved. And now your spirit is so weary that you don't want to move. You have thoughts of giving it all up, letting chaos rule. You just don't have it in yourself to make it all work anymore.

Don't despair! God is your helper. He made you and will help you. His spirit is fresh and new, and He can renew a right spirit within you. Come to Him. Let Him bring new light into your life, and let Him work miracles for you. Give up the struggle by giving it to Him. Pray on His word, and let Him lead you into greener pastures.

Your vow to God . . .

O God, please take my weary soul, transform it, and renew a right spirit within me. Take my pain and the tiredness and turn them into pleasure and joy. Remind me with the wisdom of Your word, and revive me with the energy of Your love. You are the reason in this world. Thank You for Your cool water on my parched soul.

They are of the world. Therefore they speak *as* of the world, and the world hears them.

We are of God. He who knows God hears us; he who is not of God does not hear us. By this we know the spirit of truth and the spirit of error.

(1 JOHN 4:5–6)

"Whoever comes to Me and hears My sayings and does them, I will show you whom he is like:

"He is like a man building a house, who dug deep and laid the foundation on the rock. And when the flood arose, the stream beat vehemently against that house, and could not shake it, for it was founded on the rock."

(LUKE 6:47–49)

We know that we are of God, and the whole world lies under the sway of the wicked one.

(1 JOHN 5:19)

The world would have you believe that you are nothing unless you make a lot of money or look like a model or act perfect all the time. The world would have you believe that you are nothing without that man who does you wrong. The world would have you believe that there isn't anything to live for except the empty, hollow life that the world has created.

But the world is full of lies. Jesus commanded you to be in the world, but not of it. Do not be seduced by the false gods around you. Keep your eyes focused on the mission for which you have been sent here by God. You don't need to sell your soul to the world to find pleasure—Jesus bought your soul with His blood, and holds your heart in the palm of His hand. He is the Way, the Truth and the Light. The way of the world is death, but the way of Jesus Christ is new and everlasting life.

Your vow to God . . .

I reject the lies of the world, and I embrace the truth of You. Jesus, You are my redeemer and my salvation. I know that I can only enter Heaven through You, and knowing You is like heaven for me. I believe You, and I know that You have made me into exactly the woman You want me to be.

Worry

Why be like the pagans who are so deeply concerned about these things? Your heavenly Father already knows your needs, and he will give you all you need from day to day if you live for him and make the kingdom of God your primary concern.

(MATTHEW 6:32–33[+])

Cease from anger, and forsake wrath;
Do not fret—*it* only *causes* harm.

For evildoers shall be cut off;
But those who wait on the Lord,
They shall inherit the earth.

(PSALM 37:8–9)

The Lord is my light and my salvation—
    so why should I be afraid?
The Lord protects me from danger—
    so why should I tremble?

(PSALM 27:1[+])

When you worry, you fill up your mind with thoughts of negativity, what-ifs and panic. The worry squeezes you further and further until the very thing you are worrying about becomes so huge in your mind that your whole life depends on it. You become consumed by fear. And if you aren't worrying enough, you reason, then there's something wrong. You begin to worry that you *aren't* worrying.

Isn't this silly? It's also dangerous. It means that we aren't trusting God enough to carry out the promises that He has made. Yes, He has given you responsibilities, and it's important to treat those responsibilities carefully. But God has commanded us to trust Him. Remember when Jesus rebuked His disciples who had such little faith? Become a woman of faith, not a woman of fear. Faith is more becoming of the Lord's lady.

YOUR VOW TO GOD . . .

I release worry and embrace my faith in You. I know that You have never failed me—not even once—and I know that You never will. I move from fear to faith, from doubt to trust. You are my Lord, and I am Your lady.

Wailing Women's Prayer Pages

Troubles I Have

Lord, I am having trouble accepting the changes occurring in my life. . . .

_____

_____

_____

_____

_____

_____

_____

_____

_____

_____

_____

_____

_____

_____

_____

Lord, please help me.

Trophies I Have Received

Lord, You have helped me. . . .

_____

_____

_____

_____

_____

_____

_____

_____

_____

_____

_____

_____

_____

Thank You, my Lord.

Troubles I Have

Lord, I am having trouble with my marriage. . . .

_____

_____

_____

_____

_____

_____

_____

_____

_____

_____

_____

_____

_____

_____

_____

Lord, please help me.

Trophies I Have Received

Lord, You have helped me. . . .

_____

_____

_____

_____

_____

_____

_____

_____

_____

_____

_____

_____

_____

_____

_____

_____

_____

Thank You, my Lord.

Troubles I Have

Lord, I am having trouble with my children. . . .

_____

_____

_____

_____

_____

_____

_____

_____

_____

_____

_____

_____

_____

_____

Lord, please help me.

Trophies I Have Received

Lord, You have helped me. . . .

_____

_____

_____

_____

_____

_____

_____

_____

_____

_____

_____

_____

_____

_____

_____

Thank You, my Lord.

Troubles I Have

Lord, I am having trouble forgiving. . . .

_____

_____

_____

_____

_____

_____

_____

_____

_____

_____

_____

_____

_____

_____

Lord, please help me.

Trophies I Have Received

Lord, You have helped me. . . .

_____

_____

_____

_____

_____

_____

_____

_____

_____

_____

_____

_____

_____

_____

_____

Thank You, my Lord.

Troubles I Have

Lord, I am having trouble in my relationships. . . .

_____

_____

_____

_____

_____

_____

_____

_____

_____

_____

_____

_____

_____

_____

Lord, please help me.

Trophies I Have Received

Lord, You have helped me. . . .

_____
_____
_____
_____
_____
_____
_____
_____
_____
_____
_____
_____
_____
_____
_____

Thank You, my Lord.

Troubles I Have

Lord, I am having trouble with my finances. . . .

_____

_____

_____

_____

_____

_____

_____

_____

_____

_____

_____

_____

_____

_____

Lord, please help me.

Trophies I Have Received

Lord, You have helped me. . . .

_____

_____

_____

_____

_____

_____

_____

_____

_____

_____

_____

_____

_____

_____

Thank You, my Lord

Troubles I Have

Lord, I am having trouble coping with the loss of a loved one. . . .

_____

_____

_____

_____

_____

_____

_____

_____

_____

_____

_____

_____

_____

Lord, please help me

Trophies I Have Received

Lord, You have helped me. . . .

_____

_____

_____

_____

_____

_____

_____

_____

_____

_____

_____

_____

_____

_____

Thank You, my Lord.

Troubles I Have

Lord, I am having trouble accepting disappointment. . . .

_____

_____

_____

_____

_____

_____

_____

_____

_____

_____

_____

_____

_____

_____

_____

Lord, please help me.

Trophies I Have Received

Lord, You have helped me. . . ,

_____

_____

_____

_____

_____

_____

_____

_____

_____

_____

_____

_____

_____

_____

Thank You, my Lord.

Troubles I Have

Lord, I am having trouble controlling my anger. . . .

_____

_____

_____

_____

_____

_____

_____

_____

_____

_____

_____

_____

_____

_____

Lord, please help me.

Trophies I Have Received

Lord, You have helped me. . . .

_____

_____

_____

_____

_____

_____

_____

_____

_____

_____

_____

_____

_____

_____

Thank You, my Lord.

Troubles I Have

Lord, I am having trouble at work. . . .

_____

_____

_____

_____

_____

_____

_____

_____

_____

_____

_____

_____

_____

_____

_____

_____

Lord, please help me.

Trophies I Have Received

Lord, You have helped me. . . .

_____

_____

_____

_____

_____

_____

_____

_____

_____

_____

_____

_____

_____

Thank You, my Lord.

Troubles I Have

Lord, I am having trouble with my self-image. . . .

_____

_____

_____

_____

_____

_____

_____

_____

_____

_____

_____

_____

_____

_____

Lord, please help me.

Trophies I Have Received

Lord, You have helped me. . . .

_____

_____

_____

_____

_____

_____

_____

_____

_____

_____

_____

_____

_____

_____

Thank You, my Lord.

Troubles I Have

Lord, I am having trouble letting go of past hurts. . . .

_____

_____

_____

_____

_____

_____

_____

_____

_____

_____

_____

_____

_____

_____

_____

Lord, please help me.

Trophies I Have Received

Lord, You have helped me. . . .

_____

_____

_____

_____

_____

_____

_____

_____

_____

_____

_____

_____

_____

_____

Thank You, my Lord.

Coming soon in hardcover

T.D.Jakes

author of THE LADY, HER LOVER, AND HER LORD

MAXIMIZE
THE
MOMENT

God's Action Plan for Your Life

Putnam